Praise for *The Art of Is*

"Stephen Nachmanovitch's *The Art of Is* is ... tion on living, living fully, living in the present. To the author, an improvisation is a co-creation that arises out of listening and mutual attentiveness, out of a universal bond of sharing that connects all humanity. It is a product of the nervous system, bigger than the brain and bigger than the body; it is a once-in-a-lifetime encounter, unprecedented and unrepeatable. Drawing from the wisdom of the ages, *The Art of Is* not only gives the reader an inside view of the states of mind that give rise to improvisation, it is also a celebration of the power of the human spirit, which — when exercised with love, immense patience, and discipline — is an antidote to hate."

— **Yo-Yo Ma,** cellist

"In an age of standardized packages and constrained choices, Stephen Nachmanovitch gives us *The Art of Is*, a refreshing encounter with how to improvise and be fully alive in the face of deadening habits of mind. The author is a musician and a teacher who has an uncanny ability to see and listen and help others do likewise. We are verbs, not nouns, he tells us, because we are ever in motion — open to change and surprise. Like musicians who improvise together, human beings can break barriers: teaching, playing, creating, and being present to one another. In clear prose, Nachmanovitch effortlessly shows how people discover — in themselves — the sheer power to relate and endlessly adapt."

— **Jerry Brown,** governor of California
1975–1982 and 2011–2018

"*The Art of Is* IS real ART! It is so lucid, grand, kind, easygoing, and deeply helpful, I could not stop reading it, even in time I did not 'have'! It is full of surprises, gems, and open-ended inspirations. It starts from the moment of Mahalia Jackson's startling outburst to MLK Jr., catapulting his "I have a dream" speech into the improvisation of a soaring liberation of the spirit that it was. Stephen Nachmanovitch takes us with him on his life-walk of love in music all over the world. He delivers us to a place of new vitality in our own lives where we more fully recognize the harmonies at hand. This is a lovely guidebook for our own journeys, helping us appreciate ourselves and each other as the precious human beings endowed with liberty and opportunity that we are!"

— **Robert Thurman,** Jey Tsong Khapa Professor of Buddhist Studies, Columbia University, co-founder of Tibet House

"A beautiful book, full of power, full of life, written from the deep experience of an artist and a wise person."

— **Joan Halifax,** abbot, Upaya Zen Center

"Stephen Nachmanovitch brings forty years of practicing improv to the page and offers a rich trove, hard-won and long-pondered. In graceful prose that reflects not only his talking the talk but walking the walk, he explores the art of being present. You'll finish the book enriched by his experiences studying under Zen masters and his mentor, the great polymath Gregory Bateson, and teaching aspiring improvisers all over the world."

— **Randy Fertel,** author of *A Taste for Chaos: The Art of Literary Improvisation*

"Stephen Nachmanovitch beautifully reveals a world of communication and co-creation that is both new and ancient. To play in this realm of improvisation is to recognize the tenderness with which interdependence knows aloneness, and the way silence defines sound. The stories he tells show us that the complexity and simplicity of life itself exist in our interrelationships. These findings are laid out in this book with grace, humor, and careful articulation. Nachmanovitch makes it clear that the art of being human now is acutely tied into an improvisational way of being: making sense of ourselves, each other, and the natural world in ways that find new offerings within old patterns. It is to feel anew."

— **Nora Bateson,** filmmaker, International Bateson Institute

"*The Art of Is* gives us a precious philosophical prescription for engaging the creative opportunities of our life as the greatest work of art."

— **Alex Grey,** artist

THE
ART
of
IS

Also by Stephen Nachmanovitch

Free Play: Improvisation in Life and Art

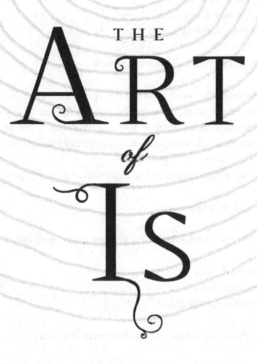

THE ART OF IS

of

IMPROVISING AS A WAY OF LIFE

STEPHEN NACHMANOVITCH

New World Library
Novato, California

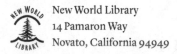

New World Library
14 Pamaron Way
Novato, California 94949

Text design by Tona Pearce Myers

Library of Congress Cataloging-in-Publication data is available.

First printing, April 2019
ISBN 978-1-60868-615-5
Ebook ISBN 978-1-60868-616-2

Printed in Canada on 100% postconsumer-waste recycled paper

New World Library is proud to be a Gold Certified Environmentally Responsible Publisher. Publisher certification awarded by Green Press Initiative. www.greenpressinitiative.org

10   9   8   7   6   5   4   3   2

For my dear ones, Leslie, Jack, and Greg

*and in memory of Gregory Bateson, who taught me that
beauty is recognizing the pattern that connects*

•   •   •

Contents

III. ART AND POWER

Sometimes we blur the distinction between art and life; sometimes we try to clarify it. We don't stand on one leg. We stand on both.

— John Cage

It takes two to know one.

— Gregory Bateson

Tell Them About
the Dream

On August 28, 1963, at the Lincoln Memorial, during the climax of the March on Washington for Jobs and Freedom, the great gospel singer Mahalia Jackson was sitting on the platform near her friend Martin Luther King. Dr. King had begun reading his prepared address. Seven paragraphs into the speech, Jackson broke in and shouted, "Tell them about the dream, Martin! Tell them about the dream!"

King pushed aside his notes and began improvising.

His written text did not mention dreams. As he looked up at the crowd and rolled into the rhythmic majesty of "I have a dream," Dr. King was riffing on part of an earlier speech he had given at Cobo Hall in Detroit but that he felt had not worked very well; he was riffing on bits from the Bible, from Shakespeare, from Lincoln, from the Constitution and the Declaration of Independence. The ghost of Gandhi was never far. Though we can identify the deep roots of King's words, the innumerable strands and influences had been collectively digested, absorbed, and integrated. The interbeing of many is expressed in the voice of each of us. We recognize King's courage and brilliance, but he was not some solitary genius spinning "creativity" out of whole cloth. There are no such geniuses. This is what it is to be human: to learn and assimilate the patterns of culture, community, and environment, both conscious and unconscious, and alter them as needed, make them ours, so that the voice spontaneously emerging is our voice, interdependent with the human world in which we live. Thus we breathe life into art and art into life.

Improvising means coming prepared, but not being attached to the preparation. Everything flows into the creative act in progress. Come prepared, but be willing to accept interruptions and invitations. Trust that the product of your preparation is not your papers and plans, but yourself. Know that no solo is solo: even one of the greatest speeches of the twentieth century was helped into existence by a good friend's blurted reminder.

·

Introduction

I have been a professional improviser for more than forty years. I've taught workshops from Germany to Argentina to Japan. I've played a black electric violin in a Buddhist temple, and a three-century-old viola d'amore in the Large Hadron Collider. This book is the trace of decades spent traveling around collaborating with, teaching, and learning from ever-widening circles of people. It has grown from playing with music, words, movement, images, and even computer code, learning about the forms and interdependent patterns of play. Such play is a way not only of connecting with people but of discovering the connections that were already present but unsuspected.

Those of us who gravitate toward improvisational music do so because we enjoy relating to other human beings as equals. That is the core of the experience for me. That is the chief relevance of our practice for the world beyond art. Our work, at its most genuine, can bring us into a living model of social openness through the practice of listening. In a world where people are prone to retreating into academic, aesthetic, and professional cubbyholes, where people are divided by the fault lines of very real racial, gender, and economic inequity, there is an ever-pressing need for this kind of practice.

When asked to define *improvising*, I say I play music that is less than five minutes old. Yet it is ancient, in that the sounds that attract me have an archaic feel. When it is truly *happening* I feel I am lightly touching something deep in culture, deep in genetics, deep in our animal nature — a fundamental connection to others. Making art, whether you do it solo or in a group, derives its patterns from everything around us, in an interdependent network. We learn to work as nature does, with the material of ourselves: our body, our mind, our companions, and the radical possibilities of the present moment.

In my twenties I met another young American, a Zen Buddhist priest. He spoke of doing zazen — sitting meditation — as practice. The word *practice* is consistently used to describe meditative activity; I had heard and read it many times before, but that day, for some reason, it hit me between the eyes. I am a musician, I thought, and now I know what practice is. Music, dance, sports, medicine, sitting still on a cushion in a state of concentrated awareness: all are forms of practice, skilled disciplines of doing and being what you are rather than some preparatory work to get to a goal. So began for me a lifelong exploration of the Buddha dharma, the Tao, and other traditions East and West that link up to artistic practice. And with a Buddhist perspective, I began to link improvising with the other imps: impermanence and imperfection. I learned to relish these essential qualities of life and art. And above all, I came to see art-making not as a matter of displaying skill but of awakening and realizing altruistic intentions.

When I was even younger, I was sure I was going to be a biologist. Then a psychologist. I was fascinated by living organisms: bodies, minds, social relations, play. The first article I ever published was in the *Journal of Protozoology*. I was enthralled by how a single cell can perform all of life's essential activities, sustain itself in an environment, swim, hunt, interact with others. That protean quality of life is still what guides me as an artist: creating music without dividing into separate functions of composer and performer, doing intermedia art forms such as visual music that speak to several senses at once.

Teachers in universities, conservatories, and high schools regard improvising as a fresh, mysterious item that should be included in the curriculum, if only they can figure out how to do it, earnestly trying to catch up with their students. But it is not an item in a list of skills we might check off in a syllabus. It is not a style or form, not a department or specialty. Improvising is life itself.

What I offer in the following chapters, from different angles and aspects, laced with journeys into music, art, science, politics, business, philosophy, pottery — are glimpses into moments of human contact. These glimpses may take place in the relatively safe and tame environment of a classroom, but later we will meet Herbert Zipper, who was able to cultivate them in the living hell of a Nazi concentration camp. We'll visit John Cage's living room, where we will discuss the merits of noisy refrigerators and discover the resonance between mushrooms and music. We'll learn what we can from frogs. We'll meet an experimental musician who becomes mayor of a small town and changes it for the better. We'll unearth the connection between Clint Eastwood's hat and Japanese folk pottery. And we'll see how an old koan about a priestess who defends herself from assault with a slip of paper she manifests into a sword speaks to our duty as artists and free human beings.

Throughout these diverse settings, similar themes and lessons crop up and repeat. Improvising cannot be understood as merely a musical or theatrical technique. It must be examined from multiple perspectives, turned over again and again, to reveal their commonality. We examine many types of moments because the crucial lesson of this book is that artistic power is available to anyone, at any moment. It is not a psychological tool, or an artistic tool. It is a way of being.

This book is about what happens in the moments and spaces between people when we create together. Music, movement, image, words are experienced as physiological, as unforced as breathing or the circulation of blood. Such experience is possible not only in the arts but in medicine, in teaching, in civic engagement — anywhere we like. This intimacy doesn't happen all the time; it comes to an end, and mundane pursuits take over. But when it happens, it is a form of magic and bliss. We co-create something that arises out of listening and mutual attentiveness. We discover that the nervous system is bigger than the brain, bigger than the body.

The most ordinary act of creativity is spontaneous conversation — the art of listening and responding, interacting, taking in environmental factors unconsciously but with precision, modifying what we do as a result of what we see and hear, touch and make, a multidimensional feedback. In our daily lives we create and recognize connections all the time.

We don't need extraordinary credentials. There is nothing special about it, but from that nothing arises our opportunity to attain some wisdom and compassion about the world in which we live. And so we can take art off the pedestal and put it where it belongs, in the dynamic center of our lives.

•

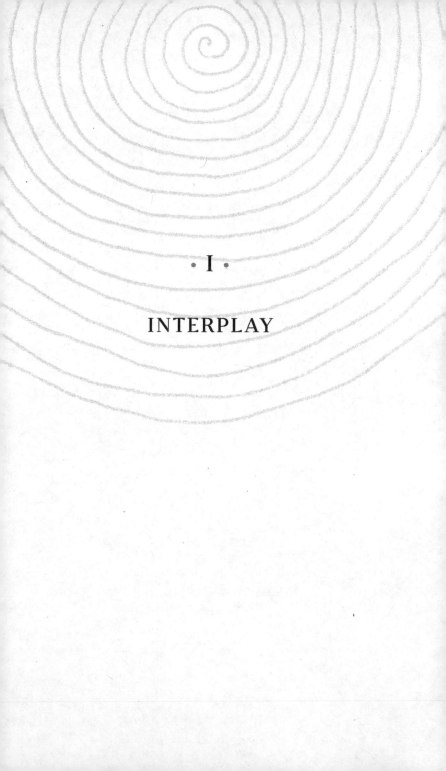

· I ·

INTERPLAY

Improvising

*I am interested in what happens to people who
find the whole of life so rewarding that they are
able to move through it with the same kind of
delight in which a child moves through a game.*
— Margaret Mead

An improvisation by a small group of musicians is a micro-
cosm of evolution. It grows from seemingly nothing, from
what appear to be random elements of the environment, and
self-organizes into a distinctive event with its own shape,
with feeling and relevance. A leaderless ensemble coop-
erates, exchanging signals of give-and-take, stimulus and
response, mutual respect and playfulness. No one is giving
directions, yet people find a way to come together in a clear
and compelling pattern of action. Paying exquisite attention
to each other, they find form and refine its development.
They invent a language and culture from the ground up.

As I work with groups in this ancient art, no matter how
often I have seen it, I continue to be stunned by how easy it is,
and how high the quality of the result. The music composes
itself. Sound and movement, gesture and word, story and
color, pattern and structure emerge through the ordinary

means of communication and feedback at which we are all unconsciously adept.

In a workshop in Canada, four young drama students perform a brief piece, surrounded by twenty-five others in a circle of support. The quartet plays together in vocal sounding and movement. Bodies interweave through space as dynamic sculpture. Nothing is discussed beforehand, but a long conversation ensues afterward. The students discuss the imagery that came up, their communication with each other, how they spontaneously partnered in developing metaphor and complete expression of body and mind in the confines of this big, open studio. One person says he imagined the performers' bodies as earth and water, feeling the piece connected them not only to those of us in the room but also to nature as seen out the big windows and beyond, to the news of war and political insanity, of which they were acutely aware. From there they discuss their interdependence within the studio as a way into the interdependence of all human beings with each other and with our natural and social environment, cutting through racial, national, professional, and age barriers. The discussion, which began as an exchange of observations about what happened in the piece, has jumped to issues of global survival. I stand in amazement watching this conversation evolve. Another participant says, "Out of animosity comes collaboration." In the play-space of that room, they are modeling something foundational for the world.

Don't let *anyone* tell you the arts are just a frill — some sideshow to the main events of life.

• • •

I drive through the intersection of two busy freeways, connected by a weave lane — a single lane on the right-hand side for both incoming and exiting traffic. The entering and exiting cars weave across each other's paths — always dangerous, calling for hyperalertness. However, there are very few accidents — most people negotiate the merging of incoming and outgoing traffic safely. One day I was trying to veer off the freeway just as a large yellow truck was merging on. We were communicating with each other in split seconds, responding to ever-changing conditions. The driver of the yellow truck and I were performing a duo improvisation. When musicians or actors play together, when people converse in daily life, we are cueing each other through subtle channels of facial expression, posture, gesture, rhythm of movement, tone of voice, a tiny nod of the head. In freeway traffic we mostly communicate through changes in the velocity and momentum of large, fast-moving, blunt objects. Yet it works; we are able to perform this dance many times a day. Constrained by the architecture of the road, by the rules of traffic, people need to pay exquisitely close attention to each other. Traffic is strangely like jazz — people doing as they please but within culturally determined norms and rules. The balancing of the rules with spontaneous response, as in music, theater, dance, and sport, is mediated by instantaneous awareness of context.

Some years ago I heard that my writings about improvisation were being used in an Argentinean aviation school. This seemed surprising — one thinks of flying an airliner as a highly structured activity, in which the skills need to flow in a predictable way. Yet to get the plane to the predetermined place at the predetermined time, following the flight plan and protocols, the pilot has to absorb and react to constant interruption by the unexpected — flocks of birds, abrupt fluctuations of weather, behavior of other aircraft. He or she has to be comfortable being surprised by unforeseen events and folding that surprise into the flow of smooth activity. Interruption means having your concentration spoiled: but nothing can spoil your concentration if every change that comes into your sensorium is part of the game.

• • •

Listening to political or corporate spokespeople, we often have an intuitive sense that they are lying, even when they happen to be telling the truth. As they read their manicured scripts we sense the stilted and contrived tone, because we are used to spontaneous, interactive, face-to-face communication.

Every day we have conversations that are reasonably lucid and interesting, without needing to rehearse them. I wrote about this decades ago and have repeated the idea many times since. Each time I repeat it, I am blurring my own line between the spontaneous and the rehearsed, so I was ripe for a surprise. One day I was speaking at the University of Virginia and said, "We don't write down our conversations before we have them." Most of the students nodded in agreement, and I expected to go on with my talk. But a young woman raised her hand to interrupt. She said, "Sometimes *I* write things down before I say them." That stopped me. I asked, "Really? When?" She answered, "When I'm going to talk to a boy." For her, talking to a boy she liked was fraught with trepidation. The stakes were high. I found it fascinating because while she was admitting to her fear, at the same time she was brave enough to stand up and say this in front of two hundred people.

Perhaps the person to whom we're speaking might think we're a fool, or perhaps we're being graded or assessed. We want to nail things down so that we appear to be in control. Improvising, we might make fools of ourselves; but when we speak from a script, we also have the possibility, at least as great, of making fools of ourselves.

Blurting out the truth can be a high-risk action. Often big stakes and legitimate fears are involved. Diplomats learn to speak with circumspection because misunderstood words, especially across diverse cultures, can spark an international dispute. Who among us doesn't sometimes avoid speaking out, from politeness, from fear of failure, or simply because we forget to pay attention to our own minds? Who among us has not lied to avoid making a cruel remark?

But blurting out the truth can also result in unexpected professions of love or friendship. Blurting out the truth may lead to unexpected commitments to a life project. Blurting out the truth may lead someone to quit a job in which he or she is required to do something dishonorable — causing short-term havoc in the person's life but perhaps improving just a little bit the lives of others. Often playing a musical instrument or dancing allows us to make such statements more directly, getting to even deeper truths and patterns than we can reach with speech. The language of body and action may teach us a simpler way to do things and reveal knowledge we had within us but had not suspected. Dreams, the royal road to the unconscious, are sometimes a way of blurting out the truth, in images, metaphors, and connections that give rise to creative breakthroughs in our life and work.

Art is the act of balancing: knowing what to prepare, what to leave to the moment, and the wisdom to know the difference.

• • •

Composer Phillip Bimstein moved from Chicago to a small town, Springdale, Utah, to live in the beauty of nature and concentrate on his work. But somehow he found himself drawn into local affairs and was elected to two terms as mayor of Springdale. This town was so rife with conflict that the previous mayor found dead chickens thrown on his front lawn by irate citizens. Bimstein discovered that he could use his experience as an improviser and composer to facilitate communication in town, and he dramatically changed local politics for the better. Certain principles of listening and mutual respect pervade music making, whether in small groups or symphony orchestras. If you can't hear what your fellow musicians are playing, you are playing too loud. People become attuned through practice to listening to each other, listening to the environment. In music, contrasting themes and emotions blend — not necessarily harmonizing or agreeing, but weaving together in exposition and development. "When musicians improvise together the interaction between them is as collaborative and communicative as it gets. Improvisation brings out not only individual expressions, but collective efforts to build something together." Bimstein found himself facilitating, and bearing witness to, a small community "composing and performing a new democracy." He describes the development of a new collaborative tone in town meetings, used in resolving disputes over real estate and city services. He learned how to be a conductor, allowing consonant and dissonant combinations of voices to move together without squelching individual voices. In a 1997 article, *Parade* magazine called Bimstein "The Man Who Brought Civility Back to Town." Living is art, and living together with people who are not just like us is *really* art, perhaps the most important art.

· · ·

In the Theatres Act of 1843, the British Parliament criminalized improvisation. All performances had to pass through the filter of state censorship, and theater managers were required to submit an advance copy of the script to the Lord Chamberlain's Office. Unscripted theater could not be predicted and controlled. This law was eventually overturned — but not until 1968!

· · ·

I value what I have learned as an improviser, but improvising in itself has no value. Plenty of amoral demagogues are fluent improvisers. History, right up to this day, presents us with examples of tyrants deft at spinning stories, modulating frames of reference, using imagery and emotional rhetoric to incite fear and hatred in a crowd. Such manipulators, ranging from showmen, salesmen, and petty politicians to brutal, violent dictators, are often skilled at spontaneous speech that, like art, touches the interface between our conscious and unconscious perceptions. Like actors, such people often have more control over their facial expressions, tone, timing, and other communicational qualities than is good for them, or for the rest of the world. We can be fascinated and entranced by the sound of poison pouring into our ears.

Creation has an essential ethical dimension. We often conflate creativity with cleverness, or with superficial innovation. Defining the ethical matrix that separates creativity from destructiveness is notoriously difficult, but it has something to do with recognizing our kinship with each other and with the natural world we inhabit. We can begin by cultivating the activity of the drama students we encountered at the beginning of this chapter — mutual respect.

• • •

Del Close, one of the gurus of instant theater, said that your job as an improviser is not to come up with clever lines but to make your partner's shitty line sound good. Keith Johnstone describes this principle using the wonderfully old-fashioned word *chivalry*. This is something we seldom see in the public sphere: mutual respect, mutual support, building something together that we might never have dreamt of on our own. Improvising is all about human relationship. It is about listening, responding, connecting, and being generous. When a group of free players gets together and unfolds a coherent and interesting piece without a prior plan or template, it is like watching separate beings become integrated into a single nervous system. It is a partnership, with each other and with the audience, in the deepest sense of the word. I even get this feeling when I am playing or hearing a solo improvisation. Each tone and gesture can be seen as an invitation to deepen the information and feelings that are unfolding. The discipline of improvisation involves sensing invitations, accepting them, and supporting each other. There is not much room to be egotistical or greedy for attention. Leadership might be clearly visible at one moment and subtler at others, but it is fluid and shared; it slides around from person to person, like a fugue. We are able to engage in the give-and-take of communication. Exchange, flow, listening, responding: our improvising can become a mini-economy, a mini-ecology, a template, in fact, for a self-organizing, organic form of democracy.

Artistic creativity won't heal the horrors of the world; it won't save anyone or anything. But it is practice — and through practice we change the self, and the relationship of the self with all things.

. . .

Union organizers have a technique for bringing a factory to a standstill without actually going on strike. It is called an obedience strike, or work-to-rule. Quite simply, the workers follow every rule and regulation to the letter. We're going to do our job exactly as it is stipulated. The problem is that no one can design a formula, job description, or software algorithm for every contingency. Soon everything grinds to a halt. If management wants to frustrate the work-to-rule action, they have to command the workers as follows: you *must* interpret your jobs freely, using personal judgment about each case based on context. What a marvelous double bind! "The letter killeth, but the spirit giveth life" — one of the most practical statements in the Bible.

. . .

The pioneering theater and film director Peter Brook pointed out that in the days of Ibsen and Chekhov, people went to the theater to see well-written plays acted out with the magic of lights, sets, costumes, and so forth. Today, with movies and TV, many of those elements can be realized far better than on the stage. So what now is the function of live theater, whether improvised, composed, or a hybrid between? Brook's answer is that we go to the theater to be personally involved in an event that can only happen in this place, at this time, at this temperature, in these acoustics, with these people. We come for an experience of presence. It is that sense of concrete immediacy and impermanence that theater must provide.

The unmediated presence of players with each other, with spectators, is the true purpose of live art. A young man at one of my university workshops remarked that during the two-hour session of a hundred people playing together, he was not once tempted to take out his phone. He said that every time he was at an event that interested him, he compulsively shared photos or videos. But this time he realized that the essence of the experience was *being there*. The more our society dissolves into a mirror labyrinth of screens and telecommunication, the more vital is the experience of simply being with each other.

There is such a ferment of artistic exploration today, occurring almost entirely below the radar of both mass media and high-culture media. These encounters bring forward the element of music that is more important than sound, of theater that is more important than story, of art that is more important than imagery. That element is people, interacting and present for each other. At each moment we are there to witness an event that has never taken place before and will never take place again. This is true not only of theater but of every instance in life. The key to creativity is other human beings. As we realize this in our day-to-day practice, our art becomes, in the words of the musician and scholar George Lewis, a power stronger than itself.

• • •

There is a word from the South African Bantu language, *ubuntu:* mutual humanity. In the related Zulu/Xhosa language, they say, "*Umuntu ngumuntu ngabantu.*" "I am a person through your being a person." *Ubuntu* is intimately related to Buddhist ideas of interdependence, and as Archbishop Desmond Tutu explains, it is the opposite of Descartes' *I think, therefore I am.* It is the opposite of our idea of the solitary genius-creator-intellect who produces masterpieces in a room.

Clarence Jones was the speechwriter and close friend who happily watched as Dr. King pushed aside the text he had helped prepare. Jones reports that King had used the phrase *I have a dream* in a previous speech with little effect on the audience. That day in August of 1963 was different. "The power is not in the words themselves. Nor is it in the speaker. The power was woven into the feedback loop that jumped between the words, the speaker, and his audience."

Ubuntu is that feedback, looping around to weave a network of reciprocity. Doris Lessing called it "substance-of-we-feeling" — awareness and sensation flowing throughout the body and between self and others and environment. We think the body is in the body and the mind is in the head, but actually, down the pathways of communication, through our limbs, and the instruments with which we extend ourselves, through the resonance of a room as sounds return to us, it is all an indissoluble continuum of conversation.

Art activates empathy, and creates the opportunity for it, inviting us to see for a while through someone else's personality and experience. Gregory Bateson said, "It takes two to know one." We know ourselves through each other. That is why, if you stand up and play a solo, as a storyteller, dancer, actor, or musician, you are still operating in this infinite nexus of relationship, listening and responding. We come to see individual and collective experience on a continuum, just as improvisation and composition occur on a continuum. We become stewards of these newly discovered relationships with our partners and our environment. With practice we can make those relationships richer, more interesting, more generous.

Improvising makes visible some truths of daily life that we experience but seldom think about: that we can navigate our way through complex systems in the simple act and art of listening and responding; that creativity is the property of everyone and not just of a chosen few; that the ordinary, everyday mind is expressive and creative. From this magical interaction the work is born.

Verbs and Nouns

The spotted hawk swoops by and accuses me,
he complains of my gab and my loitering.
I too am not a bit tamed, I too am untranslatable,
I sound my barbaric yawp over the roofs of the world.
— Walt Whitman

I was in London for a few days before traveling to a conference on improvisation in Wales. I walked along the South Bank of the Thames, taking in the sun and puffy clouds reflected on the water, gulls wheeling and yawping overhead, and crowds of mostly happy-looking people strolling up and down the walkways, each involved in his or her personal mixture of business and pleasure. I was supposed to give the keynote talk at the conference, which gathered international improvisers from across the arts, including musicians, theater people, dancers, visual artists, filmmakers, educators, psychologists, and others, for a series of talks and performances. While I was looking forward to this conference, as usual I didn't have the foggiest idea what I was going to say. As a practicing improviser I have grown used to this cloud of unknowing, and to discovering that when the day arrives, the talk will organize itself. But at a certain phase in between, I dissolve into a panic: *this* time I will have nothing to say, or it will be a confused jumble. I will get up and make a fool of myself.

Last time I was in London, years before, the South Bank was a grungy area of decayed industrial buildings. Now it had been transformed for the new millennium into a miles-long environment of footpaths along the river, with galleries, theaters, and cafés sprouting off to the right. I noticed how architecture is a score for improvisation: the shaped container and guide for a buzzing ecology of individuals, families, small groups, intent business people, tourists, working men and women carrying tools, talking with their friends. The design of the outdoor space that surrounded us lent a particular flavor, a relaxed but energetic style to our collective activity. The walkways, never entirely straight, constantly varying in width and geometry, channeled the stochastic process of people's activity into a kind of dance.

I wandered into a bookstore. I randomly browsed among the shelves, not looking for anything in particular, passing the psychology section on my right. Suddenly out of the corner of my eye, I saw a book. The spine was fire-engine red, with bold white lettering that said IMPROVISING. Needless to say, I did a double take and turned back to the shelf to find the book that had caught my eye. I was eager to learn who wrote it and what he or she had to say. I scanned the shelves from top to bottom. Nothing. I searched again, thinking that perhaps I had scrambled the letters of another title. But there was no red book. I had hallucinated it. Clearly, in the workings of the unconscious, I was anticipating the improv conference; but something else was at work in that hallucination. *Improvisation* had been transformed to *improvising*. Not a noun, but a verb, in the active present.

• • •

This little hallucination encapsulated patterns and ideas that had preoccupied me for decades. Like many such experiences, it was the fast, synaptic summation of information that had always been available, hiding in plain sight. That swift connecting of patterns, flowing through time, is itself what we often mean by improvising. The gift was that I now had a focal point for the talk I was about to give.

It took me a few years more to realize that the book I had imagined in the store was *this* book.

As the vision of the book and the word *improvising* came to me, I recognized that I was stepping onto a well-trodden path. My mentor, the anthropologist and philosopher Gregory Bateson, was fond of repeating the slogan STAMP OUT NOUNS, coined by his friend and student Anatol Holt. "Language," Gregory told me, "can be a wonderful servant but a terrible master." Nouns break the world and our experience apart, into *things*. Naming, and manipulating names and symbols, has enabled the lion's share of our advanced civilization. But in our love of and reliance on language, we tend to confuse the name with the thing named. Bateson often quoted the mathematician and philosopher Alfred Korzybski, who famously said, "The map is not the territory." The menu is not the meal.

• • •

The general and president Ulysses S. Grant was not the sort of person we would expect to find in an exploration of art, improvisation, and philosophy. But as he was dying of throat cancer in 1885, he spoke of the relationship between consciousness and his diminishing body functions. He said,

"The fact is, I think I am a verb instead of a personal pronoun. A verb is anything that signifies to be; to do; or to suffer. I signify all three." He came to see his body and mind as more of a process than a thing. Grant's was a view of death, a time of obvious transition, but the rest of day-to-day life is like this too; we're simply not as conscious of it. R. Buckminster Fuller, riffing on Grant's statement, said, "I live on Earth at present, and I don't know what I am. I know that I am not a category. I am not a thing — a noun. I seem to be a verb, an evolutionary process — an integral function of Universe."

• • •

Christopher Small, a musicologist strongly influenced by Bateson, suggested that people fundamentally distort music by treating it as a thing; he wanted to get rid of the noun *music* and replace it with the verb *to music*, or *musicking*. Musicking is the real-time activity of grabbing instruments and playing, singing, writing, hearing, tapping on kitchen utensils, dancing. At the moment of listening to a concert, recording, or broadcast, people are linked in participation with others near and far, including the performers. Musicking reframes song as an activity taking place in a particular time and context; it is a process.

Music (or art, literature, theater, science, technology) is often treated as a collection of works arranged on a historical timeline. The scores are regarded as having not only an independent existence but a higher existence than the performances. In the classical music world, history stretches out like a clothesline, with sheets of music notation hanging from it. We sometimes call sheet music *the music*, whereas it is just a symbolic representation, a helpful aid to communication. The noun *music* also implies an abstract Platonic

entity somewhere up in the ether, where the perfect interpretation exists. We treat the notation or the abstraction as
more real than reality. Beethoven's *music* becomes a mental
deity. But in reality Beethoven's *music*, represented on paper,
is the archaeological relic of Beethoven's *musicking*, a warm
human creating, writing, playing, singing, raging in frustration, scratching out notations he didn't like and writing
more, exploding in joy. The editing of a composition, a book,
or an architectural drawing is similarly the interactivity of a
warm human body in space and time, though the end result
may look like a solid object.

Small reminds us that the worlds of popular music likewise turn experiences into objects, and into interchangeable
commodities. And so it is in many areas of life. Teaching
becomes a curriculum validated by standardized testing,
another *thing* to be *attained*. Anything we might do can be
reified as a thing or lived as a process. Thus, we need to engage those present-tense, active verbs as antidotes to thingness: *improvising, musicking, teaching, playing, creating, being.*

· · ·

In the 1970s Augusto Boal (the first professional improviser
to be nominated for a Nobel Peace Prize) taught a round of
theater workshops in Northern Ireland, which at that time
was still violently torn apart by sectarian strife. Participants
played scenes drawn from their daily lives. Ethnic politics,
distinctions between who's in and who's out, seemed ines-
capable, even though these were people who had volunteered
for this type of open and shared experience. Boal described
how he could virtually see *Protestant* or *Catholic* stamped on
each person's forehead. Yet each side could *play*, as drama or
comedy, *with* the common concerns of family and survival in

a tough society, the personal problems that everyone shares. "We should not stamp the name of people's religions on their foreheads, instead we must try to see the person. To see people without captions!"

• • •
• • •
• • •

How wide the Gulf & Unpassable! between
Simplicity & Insipidity.

— William Blake

The phrase "thinking outside the box" arose from a famous problem in cognitive psychology, in which you are shown nine dots arranged in a grid and asked to draw four lines that connect all nine dots, without lifting your pencil. There are a number of solutions, all of which require drawing lines that stick out beyond the imaginary boundary of the square pattern. Quite often we restrict ourselves by seeing the square-that-is-not-there and don't even think of allowing our pencil to venture into the space around it. "Thinking outside the box" came to refer to thinking, behaving, or perceiving that is not conventional, that is not hackneyed, stereotyped, or robotic. But after being used for years, it has become a hackneyed, stereotyped, robotic cliché. It is a self-canceling message.

Creativity. Innovation. Vision. A generation ago these words were charged with meaning. Now they have become rancid, insipid, and banal. Overuse, and deliberate misuse as marketing buzzwords, have rendered them into cheap commodities with a limited shelf life. When something is described as "cutting-edge," you just know it's going to be dull.

Christopher Small's verb *musicking*, a freshener of our ideas, attitudes, and enjoyment as participants and listeners, has been adopted to an increasing degree by scholars. But there is always the danger that, like any name of an idea, it can turn into yet another dead buzzword, joining our collection of prefigured responses.

Creativity, innovation, improvisation, the very substance of life and learning, devolve into commodities, whether through the trendy marketing lingo of corporations and political actors or the hegemonic obscurity of academic critical theory. Whole industries have sprung up around the idea of creativity, selling it in seminars. Even an activity as ephemeral as improvisation can be commodified and packaged. We invent words like "performativity" and then study them as though they were substances.

• • •

The wonderful word *gobbledygook* was coined in 1944 by the Texas businessman and politician Maury Maverick. In a memo to his employees, he banned "gobbledygook language." "Anyone using the words *activation* or *implementation* will be shot." His reference was to the turkey, "always gobbledy gobbling and strutting with ludicrous pomposity. At the end of his gobble, there was a sort of gook."

Sometimes I feel that habits of language and thought would benefit from going onto an underground conveyor belt, to return to daylight after a century. That is why I love Keith Johnstone's use of an archaic word, *chivalry*, to describe how improvisers at their best accept, build on, nourish, and amplify the ideas and imagery developed by their partners. A similar approach is often described as *"yes, and…"* — perhaps the most generative rule of improvisational theater. But *"yes, and…,"* repeated ceaselessly, has become a platitude ready for the glue factory. *Chivalry* seems like such a quaint word in these postmodern times that it is ready for some fresh duty.

• • •

When he was in school, my son Jack brought home a fairly typical English assignment concerning a piece of fiction the class had read. The teacher asked what "qualities" a character "possessed" — bravery, creativity, duplicity, and so on. We have this way of talking as though creativity or bravery were a *thing* one could *have*. Perhaps it is a fluid, such that one person could have seven ounces of it and another could have nine liters. The nouns are all right in themselves but tend to guide our thoughts to the idea that a human being is a bag with an inside and an outside and that the bag contains a collection of items or qualities. In actuality, the actions that we call creative or brave or loving or competitive are relational. Every human activity takes place in context, in a certain time and setting. We all know of people, in real life or in fiction, who are brave at one moment and cowardly at another, people who are imaginative at one moment and dull at another. That is because these words do not describe inherent traits; they describe actions and decisions. People who have experienced fear might be labeled cowardly, or simply shy, by their peers and by themselves. If we accept this label and reinforce it, reify it, we convince ourselves more and more that the label defines us. Then we really are trapped by it, boxed in by language. Instead we can work to understand that we do not exist as static entities who always respond the same way to similar scenarios. We are dynamic, ever changing, and we have the choice in any given moment to be who we think we should be.

What can we learn from improvising? There is no "take-away" that we can carry with us. There are, rather, some things we can leave behind, including the fixed idea of self as a sack with certain contents. Qualities of interaction are not things we possess; they are activities that we manifest in a particular place and time. We can see people without captions; we can allow music to unfold without attaching labels to it. We can allow our own stories to play out in the complexity of real life.

• • •

I am not a writer — I am writing. Yesterday I was not writing. I was doing dreary errands and engaging in distraction, entertainment, and memories. It is natural to write sometimes and not to write at others. Rimbaud wrote, and then he didn't write. But if I stick with nouns — "I am a writer" — then a frustrating day like yesterday would have to be framed as "writer's block" — a *disease* for which I seek a *cure*. By treating activities or states as though they were solid objects, we buy a world of trouble. We automatically say, "I *have* a disease," "I *have* a condition." This metaphor works marvelously well in the case of infectious diseases, where a disease vector like a bacterium, virus, or toxin has indeed invaded our bodies. But too frequently it is extended to contexts in which the metaphor does not apply. Pharmaceutical industries and many other industries, of course, love this metaphor of *having*. We are so easily sucked into conceiving complex relationships and systems in the framework of problem-and-solution.

We are trained to say, I *am* this, I *am* that. We may spend much of our day playing music, driving a delivery truck, treating patients in a hospital, forecasting the weather, investigating crimes, but to be pinned down and solidified by a professional identity leaves out the immense variety of every human life. We can make the jump into thinking systemically, to realizing that we are verbs, not things.

• • •

David Chadwick, one of the priests at San Francisco Zen Center, asked Shunryū Suzuki, the master who founded the center, if he could summarize Buddhism in one sentence. This was a cocky, tongue-in-cheek question because Suzuki-roshi had many times urged his students not to make a *thing* out of Buddhism. So David expected that Suzuki would refuse to answer his question. But Suzuki did answer. He said, "Everything changes."

• • •

I remember driving in the mountains above Los Angeles with my son Greg when he was one and a half. He was at the stage when language was flooding in, ceaselessly making connections. We had a long view of the winding road heading up the hillsides and open chaparral. Every time a driver passed us on the road, Greg, sitting behind me, strapped into his car seat, pointed and shouted, "Car! Car! Car!" Then to my alarm he began to wiggle out of his restraints like Houdini, the better to stand up in the back seat and shout, "Car! Car! Car!" with a musical, rising tone, speaking with his whole body, from the feet up. Babies are like this. Beyond the obvious usefulness of language, there is the joy of naming, the power of crying out, the excitement that seems to jump from the pointing finger, the dance of light between eye and object.

That beautiful act of naming is what eventually undoes — for many of us — the freshness of our baby perceptions. We learn the labels: that's a Ford, that's Malibu Canyon, that's a chair, that's a symphony, that's money. That's a person of a certain ethnic group or religion. Having the power to name and categorize, we forget the fascination of those individual experiences, and the newness of each perception, the newness of each face that confronts us. We stop looking deeply at what is in front of us. We adopt the jaded, all-knowing view of the professional and dismiss what is in front of us because we already know what it is — I've seen it all, I know it all. Often we see people's creative urges stopped in their tracks by gatekeepers so sure of what they know that there is no room for what they don't. Every profession — musician, publisher, professor, police detective, physician, builder — has built up expertise, necessary for functioning in the world. Yet every form of expertise produces a counter-condition in which we become limited by the filters. We know what's right; we know what works; we know. And therefore we sometimes cannot see what is right in front of our noses.

Keeping that balance between expertise and freshness is the practice of a lifetime. Each of us can be the baby fascinated by the new things in the world, ready to receive. If you have learned to play the violin very well, your technique can become a jail. But if you retain your childhood capacity to use the instrument as a toy, and couple that with your expertise, your technique can become anything you want it to. The baby who shouted, "Car!" was not the same baby the next day, and the day after that. The baby is a continuous transformation of moment-to-moment action: growth, evolution, change, destruction, renewal. We passed a stream of shiny cars in the canyon one minute, and moments later passed a junk heap of rusted relics.

And so the famous words of Suzuki-roshi: "If your mind is empty, it is open to everything. In the beginner's mind there are many possibilities; in the expert's mind there are few."

• • •

One evening, over a Mexican dinner in Santa Cruz, California, Gregory Bateson told me for the first time of Anatol Holt's idea for a bumper sticker that said STAMP OUT NOUNS. I was twenty-two and he was sixty-nine. We spoke of how difficult it is to change our way of thinking, to see the world as context and process rather than a set of fixed entities. By way of conclusion, he said, "You know, there is no substance," grinning with the irony of saying this while he, an enormous shaggy old Englishman at six foot five, was looming over me with a beer in his hand. A lot of substance, yet teaching me that substance was only the current appearance of an impermanent, ever-changing, interactive life. Stamping out nouns is not a call for an exotic restructuring of language; it is an invitation to see and speak about the world as active process. We can use the terms and procedures of daily life without getting stuck in them. Then we can use language with pleasure and integrity. The reduction of anything, including activities we most love, into commodities and objects, the tendency for the lava of life to be frozen into stone by language and thought, means that we need to stamp out nouns as a continuous practice. To be a verb is a full-time occupation, like breathing.

Maury Maverick's grandfather was Samuel Maverick, after whom the word *maverick* was coined. Samuel Maverick, unlike other Texas cattlemen, did not brand his cattle. Thus, a maverick was an unbranded cow or steer. The unbranded, the unlabeled, is a significant concept for us today, when business interests are relentlessly trying to impose branding on us. Branding actually refers to the cruel procedure of using a hot iron to burn a logo into the skin of an animal —

or in the days of slavery, a human being. Our right as free human beings is not to be branded. That is where improvisation in life and art meets our daily experience. Improvising means freedom from branding. Freedom of speech, freedom of thought, not having thoughts planted in us by entities not of our choosing. Part of an improviser's work is negative: stomping on nouns, stomping on dreams of polished perfection, stomping on preconceptions of how things are supposed to be. To what extent can that stomping be a dance, with its own shape, its own wild grace, its own life-giving awareness of what and who is around us? Stamp, stomp, squish. It is great exercise for the legs, the whole body, and puts a spring in your step. With twenty-six bones in each foot, twenty muscles, and more than eighty tendons and ligaments, the combinations and permutations, the fresh, invigorating styles of stomping, are nearly infinite.

Knobs and Dials

JULIET: *You kiss by the book.*
— Shakespeare

I went to the hospital for an echocardiogram. I told the technician administering it that I wanted a copy of the video files. If there was nothing wrong with my heart, then I at least wanted to be able to edit the video and make a visual music piece from it. She said, "I'm an artist too." I asked her what her art form was. I thought she was going to say that in addition to her medical job she was a painter or songwriter. Instead she patted the machine and said, "This."

Giving an echocardiogram is one of those innumerable tasks that on the surface seem objective and by the book, but in fact there is an enormous range of personal style in how the images are taken. With dozens of knobs and switches on the machine controlling contrast and many other variables in the resulting images, with variations in the placement and pressure of the sonogram sensor on the patient's body, how it is handled and moved, the possibilities for individual style are enormous, all in the attempt to produce an "objectively" clear picture of how the heart valves are functioning. She said that when she comes into the lab each morning and sees studies done by other technicians, she can instantly identify who did each study. Each has his or her own style. When she was training to do this work, her instructor called these variations *knobology*.

Such acts are not typically recognized as art, but a fundamentally artistic process is involved in tweaking knobs on a machine or tuning the performance of an engine. These adjustments are not so different from tuning words and phrases in a paragraph, mixing pigments, or playing with gradations of speed, pressure, and point of contact on a violin bow. *Knobology* is also a term of art on aircraft carriers and submarines.

Back in the days of the telegraph — a simple digital code of dots, dashes, and pauses — a telegraph operator receiving a message could tell who was on the other end of the line, perhaps hundreds of miles away, by his or her "fist." The rhythm of those digital bleeps and pauses, small variations in tempo, revealed an individual style that was unmistakable to the experienced listener. As recently as World War II, the fist of a telegraph operator enabled us to tell the difference between real messages and those sent by enemy spies. The people who received these messages could identify who was sending it by idiosyncrasies in timing. If sensitive information like "I'm in Northern France" were coded right into the message, it could be intercepted and decoded. Instead, those receiving the communication could rely on the unique telegraphic fingerprint of the agent on the other end.

The echocardiogram technician said that in an earlier part of her life she had been an accountant. Accounting is yet another field that is supposedly objective and straightforward. Yet the choices one makes in setting up and structuring a chart of accounts are not easy to define: how to categorize this or that expense; how to balance often inchoate competing interests such as profitability, viability, legality, and ethics; how to use numbers to represent truth or to obscure it. Even jobs that are nominally uncreative require constant personal interpretation and invention.

Double-entry accounting was invented by one of those Italian Renaissance polymaths, the monk Luca Pacioli. He was also responsible for much of the theory behind perspective painting. Pacioli's book *The Divine Proportion* was illustrated by Leonardo da Vinci. Accounting and perspective painting are both arts that revolve around representing a complex, multidimensional reality on a flat piece of paper. In accounting we draw a dividing line down the middle of the page, setting up a zero point so that the debits and credits reflect against each other. To this day every bank statement, every corporation's accounting, works by Pacioli's system. Similarly, perspective painting runs an imaginary line down the canvas; we orient ourselves in three-dimensional space by the frame of reference created by that line. Our brain plays with the details and contrasts, balancing the sides so that exceptional items really stick out. We draw that line and then use it to accentuate the interplay of figure and ground. This is the virtuosity of the woman in the cardiac imaging lab. She understands the mathematics and the technology inherent in the ultrasound instrument as elements of her art. She is able to do it simultaneously as a creative form and as a technological task whose results may have life-or-death consequences. The technology *depends* on her subjectivity, on her interpretation, on her practicing it as an art.

Stuck or Sticky

I once heard the Zen master Dainin Katagiri speak of the importance of not being too sticky. I never knew if Katagiri was deliberately playing with language to give us a fresh perspective, or if it was just the way his Japanese-flavored English came out. Either way, this was a fruitful poetic inversion of our usual idea of *being stuck*. Moment by moment, each of us is attracted to certain things and repelled by others; we have fears and hopes, we entertain our ideas and the ideas prevalent in our society — and we find ourselves clinging to those ideas, following our attractions and repulsions. Concepts and passions can trap us like flypaper, or rather we ourselves are the flypaper. It is easy to see ourselves as stuck in a rut at work, stuck in a way of relating to friends or loved ones. Stuck in an addiction. Stuck in an artistic habit, writer's block, speaker's block, blocked friendship, a block in the stiff muscles of one's back. A darting mind, or a mind sticking to repetitive thoughts, blocks us from sleeping or from acting. We speak of other people as stuck in prejudice, stuck in the past.

A musician I know said, "I was so stuck in my improvisations, rattling on and on in the same way, I could hardly play sometimes, I was getting so bored with it." We have practiced a craft for years — *this* is the way to do it. We may want to try it another way, but we are stuck in *this*. We have dug a groove with all our sincere practice.

Then we feel like victims of circumstance; we are *in* a situation. But invert the relationship implied in the word, and we see ourselves as actively *sticking* rather than *stuck*. *Stuck* is a passive construction, not only of language but of a person's entire reality. *Sticky* reveals that it is we who are doing the sticking, we who choose, whether consciously or unconsciously, to cling to the objects of our attractions and repulsions. Therefore we have the power to dissolve some of this glue.

• • •

There is an old story about two monks crossing a river. They meet a beautiful young woman who wants to get across but is afraid of the rushing water. One of the monks picks her up and carries her. When they reach the far shore, he puts her down, and she goes her separate way. A bit farther along the muddy road, his companion berates him for violating his monkish vows by holding a girl in his arms. The first monk replies, "I put her down at the riverbank. Are you still carrying her?"

• • •

Robert Pirsig, in *Zen and the Art of Motorcycle Maintenance*, tells of being stuck by the roadside in the wilderness, his vehicle disabled because of a screw that has rusted in place. The screw was no longer a small, cheap, generic object like hundreds of others in the machine. This particular screw was an individual phenomenon that was worth exactly everything. The whole trip narrowed down to the problem of getting that screw out. As he investigated the machine, Pirsig realized he needed to face the mental stuckness that so often accompanies the physical. "Stuckness shouldn't be avoided. It's the psychic predecessor of all real understanding." To abide in and be able to tolerate such stuckness is one of the fruits of mindfulness practice.

A century earlier, Sigmund Freud arrived at his own method of mindfulness. In 1912 he wrote a paper of practical instructions for therapists. How does a doctor do psychoanalysis without getting caught up in his or her own predispositions? If the job is attending empathetically to the pain of many people, how does one attend to each patient without getting one's own emotions stuck in their problems? And above all, how does one understand another human being without jumping to premature conclusions? Freud wrote, "One has simply to listen." He goes on to say,

> The technique is a very simple one. It disclaims the use of any special aids, even of note-taking, and simply consists in making no effort to concentrate the attention on anything in particular, and in maintaining in regard to all that one hears the same measure of calm, quiet attentiveness — of "evenly-hovering attention." For as soon as attention is deliberately concentrated, one begins to select from the material before one.... This is just what must not be done. If

one's expectations are followed in this selection there is the danger of never finding anything but what is already known.

Our contemporary practice of mindfulness is exactly this evenly hovering attention: deliberate alertness, being in the present moment without judgment, allowing the experience to unfold without critical interference, not holding on to only what we already know.

In 1817 John Keats spoke of Negative Capability: "The ability to remain within Mysteries, Uncertainties & Doubt without the irritable reaching after fact and reason." Negative Capability is the poetics of listening. It is a skill that can be cultivated through practice, and like many skills, lost again and found again.

In *The Interpretation of Dreams*, published at the dawn of 1900, Freud contrasted this open state of mind with self-clinging, critical reflection: "The whole frame of mind of a man who is reflecting is totally different from that of a man who is observing his own psychical processes." Freud used *reflecting* to mean self-critical, discursive thinking and *observing* to mean evenly hovering attention. "In reflection, there is one more psychical activity at work than the most attentive self-observation, and this is shown amongst other things by the tense looks and wrinkled forehead of a person pursuing his reflections as compared with the restful expression of a self-observer." If we wish to visualize Freud's *reflecting*, look at Rodin's famous sculpture *The Thinker*, with his gnarled, uncomfortable posture and tight brow. Rodin was inspired by Blake's illustration of a brooding bird-headed man, looking pained and unbalanced, muscles strained. For a very different view, that of *observing*, look at images of buddhas and bodhisattvas, smiling, happy, and balanced, their backs relaxed and stable: breathing.

• • • •

In 1996 my wife and I attended a week of teachings by the Dalai Lama in the Pasadena Civic Auditorium. On this occasion His Holiness was under protection by the United States Secret Service. Normally Secret Service agents are guarding a visiting foreign president giving an hour-long talk on trade, military policy, or cultural exchange, and then they are off traveling to the next engagement. But here the Dalai Lama was taking five full days to explore the Indian philosophers Nagarjuna and Shantideva, whose writings in the first millennium remain the foundation of our modern ideas of mindfulness.

The Pasadena Civic is an ornate Art Deco building from 1930, gilded patterns festooning the tall walls of the proscenium. The Dalai Lama was surrounded by dozens of sitting lamas and monks in bright saffron and maroon Tibetan robes, as well as representatives of other Buddhist traditions, arrayed in concentric semicircles, a bit like a symphony orchestra. An enormous *thangka* painting hung from the rafters above them. Contrasting with this colorful display of people and artwork stood the men in black, at intervals around the back of the stage, with curly communicators tucked behind their ears. They stood there all day long, scanning this audience of three thousand people for the remote possibility of a weapon's glint.

The Dalai Lama was speaking about being present to the minutiae of experience as a unified mind and body, about going to more and more subtle levels of consciousness, until we are fully awake and aware of everything around us. He was speaking of the simplicity and energy of a stable posture, the stability and inner quietude that enables us to listen, see, and feel clearly, to be able to act single-mindedly when other living beings need our help.

As the hours flowed on, I found myself fascinated by the Secret Service agents standing in the background. These men in dark business suits seemed to come from the opposite end of the universe. But they were actually demonstrating what the Dalai Lama was talking about. They were utterly alert, calm, observant, standing motionless for an hour at a time, after which they quietly exchanged places with each other to refresh their view. At the end of each day they seemed as relaxed as they had at the beginning. One day there was a man who was clearly not a "real" Secret Service agent; perhaps he had been pulled in from an office job. He was visibly uncomfortable, constantly shifting position, leaning up against a column. As demonstrated by this gentleman (by most of us!), it actually takes a lot of energy to stand still. Standing or sitting, not wasting energy with unnecessary effort is a skill that takes practice, which the experienced agents showed in their quiet way. They were able, as Henry Miller put it, to stand still like a hummingbird.

In Tibetan and Zen styles of meditation, one sits with half-shuttered eyes. In Japanese this is called *fusoku furi*, un-attached *and* undetached. Not open to the public world, not closed into a private world. In this way we sustain concentration and stillness while remaining fully aware of our surroundings.

· · ·

In 1980 my teacher Gregory Bateson was dying. He was in the hospital for three weeks, then the San Francisco Zen Center invited him to be there for what turned out to be his final week. Beyond the big hospital bed that had been imported, there were black-robed figures, young American men and women in long-term Zen training. Four of them would sit in meditation in the corners of the room, facing the wall, breathing slowly in time with Gregory, who had lung disease. They seemed oblivious, like human furniture, while friends and family came to visit each day, talking with each other and with Gregory. But the moment something was needed in the room, including some of the ugly things that accompany the dying process, the Zen students would pop up and do what was needed, instantly, carefully. Then they would sit again and disappear into meditation. The image of those Zen men and women came back to me sixteen years later as I watched the Secret Service agents, with their evenly hovering attention.

· · ·

In medicine the most common errors are due to premature closure — arriving at an initial diagnosis that seems to fit the case but does not encompass a deeper investigation into all the phenomena and all the patient might have to say. As institutional pressures mount up on doctors to see more patients per hour ("productivity" is one of the most unfortunate buzzwords of our age), premature closure is implicitly encouraged. The physician too eager to fill in the chart from a set list of diagnostic codes will be less likely to *see* the patient.

How often do our well-intended efforts to fix things end up making them worse? How many of us have tried to fix a mechanical item with repeated, frustrated force and ended up breaking it instead? To remain present long enough without knowing the answer, to take the time to closely examine how the parts of the machine are connected, to respect its complexity, to perceive details and relationships that are not immediately apparent, can itself be a lubricant. To remain open-eyed and open-minded, while still retaining access to the technical information we have accumulated through our years of learning, is one of those balancing acts that comes under the heading of "wisdom." Cherish peripheral vision. The activity of our nervous system, conscious and unconscious, is constantly parsing the signal-to-noise ratio. Yet signal and noise, figure and ground, need to change places from time to time. The ignored detail that seems to be nonsense or unimportant might be the crucial thing that pops up as danger, opportunity, or inspiration — playful, off-the-wall, improbable.

Psychoanalysts will tell you that the great practitioners don't interpret. This is a funny statement coming from a discipline whose most famous book is *The Interpretation of Dreams*. To pause and allow *listening* to flower is an art that takes discipline and gives material a chance to develop in surprising ways.

• • •

The practice of intent *listening*, which we will encounter in a later chapter — paying attention to birds, to water, to industrial sounds, to the human sounds around us, to our partners in conversation — seems like the easiest thing in the world. But it is amazing how much we miss. Something else is always going on amid the endless tape-loops of consciousness. Remembering, repeating, and rehearsing clog up our ability to listen. We retell our inventory of hope, fear, anger, triumph, resentment, and jokes. Once I was taking the two-hour drive from my home in Virginia up to Washington, DC, listening, or trying to listen, to an audiobook. The CDs were divided into three-minute tracks. There was a segment early on, with an especially elegant sentence that I had vaguely remembered from reading the book long ago. I wanted to catch it and taste the words. But I kept missing it. I was thinking instead about a hurtful interaction that I had had with a close friend and colleague. While the recording was playing in my car, the tape-loop of my ruptured friendship was playing in my head, the same few rueful thoughts in different combinations and permutations. Everyone gets caught playing those old tapes about mother, father, ex-lover, ex-employer. In playing these tapes we bind ourselves up in resentment or regret. I decided to try listening to the novel as a simple mindfulness exercise: just get through a three-minute segment with total attention. But I could barely make it through a minute before my inner tape snuck in and captured my consciousness. Half an hour later I was still hitting the rewind button. After an hour

I finally succeeded in getting through the three minutes of storytelling, but just barely.

In many schools of meditation, we first learn to steady ourselves by counting our breaths. Just breathe regularly, and count each exhalation, from one to ten, then start over again. If you lose count, restart from one. It seems simple to do this for a few minutes. But it can be quite challenging to get past the number three. Consciousness is often touted as the glory of the human race. Actually, it's not so hot.

• • •

Cross your arms over your chest. Simple. Now uncross them and cross them in the opposite direction. Perhaps nervous giggles break out: we feel clumsy and discover that we have formed a lifetime habit of crossing right over left or left over right. To do it the other way around feels funny, strange, uncomfortable. We get comfortable with a certain way of doing or seeing, and that becomes the universe of possibility. Now think back to how many times in the past you've lit up with the realization that life could be so much better if you changed one habit — and then discovered just how disconcerting such change can be. To create something new, you have to unmake yourself to some extent. And that can be tremendously difficult.

Freedom to act in the moment — the capacity to improvise — can liberate us, but it also terrifies us. We are often afraid of our own ability to change, our own agility. A friend who had gotten divorced said, "It's easier to keep complaining about my mother, my ex-husband. Then I can avoid taking the risk of asking that man over there to dance with me."

In artistic production, we become comfortable in our habitual styles and methods. We can stick to these patterns forever and stay assured that we know what we're doing or that we are producing a product people approve of. This is how we can become pigeonholed by our own success. As Rilke wrote,

> we're left with yesterday's
> walk and the pampered loyalty of an old habit
> that liked us so much it decided to stay, and never left.

For the monk who won't let go of the image of his partner carrying the girl across the stream, learning the rules and sticking to them provides stability and clarity in this confusing life. *This* is how one should behave. *This* is how music is played. *This* is how sentences are written. "*This*," quoting the mantra of many organizations, "*is how we do it here.*" The *this* is comfortable. We know what we are going to find there. Thus, we get stuck in conservatism and in doing as we're told.

Stickiness is not only a matter of stasis or conservatism. We can be sticky to the need to innovate or to appear to be innovating. At a music festival I attended, a fine avant-garde percussionist produced virtuosic sounds from his snare drum, reveling in extended techniques, rubbing the drumhead with jeweler's rouge, kitchen utensils, rubber balls, and plastic tubing. He got wonderfully elongated moaning sounds from the drum. Then his fingertip flicked out and hit the drumhead, making a classic snare drum stroke. It was clear from his face that he felt he had made a mistake. He had made a conventional snare drum sound and therefore wasn't being original. He quickly covered this over with more activity, in the way musicians learn to distract attention from accidents. Was it uncreative to play a recognizable, traditional sound?

Bruce Lee, the great martial artist, developed what he

called "the style of no style." He was the first to do mixed martial arts, taking the best from all styles but not adhering to any particular school. Knowing about many disciplines, he would not be confined to any of them but do what was needed according to circumstance. Following the *Tao Te Ching*, he urged his students to be like water, yielding, shifting in form, able to penetrate everywhere.

· · ·

Around 1660 Pascal said that the root of human unhappiness was our inability to sit still in a room. A recent series of studies showed that some people would rather give themselves electric shocks than spend a few minutes sitting quietly alone. Men are more likely than women to prefer electric shock to stillness. People feel impelled to skitter around, searching for entertainment or conflict. From this discomfort we generate quarrels, wars, dramas domestic and political. If we are afraid to be alone with stillness and uncertainty, life will be an endless quest for in-flight entertainment. Suffering or feeling wounded can be a mighty entertaining distraction.

The neurologist Charles Limb recorded functional MRIs of the brains of musicians while they were improvising, then again while they were playing set compositions, and compared the two. The improvising brains showed a suppression of areas involved in critical judgment and fight-flight responses. People are afraid to be patient with their own creativity, to tolerate (and enjoy!) the ambiguity of exploration. Our impulse is to drown it out with criticism. We learn this habit early. I was in the hardware store looking for a tool.

Next to me were a mother and her seven-year-old son. The boy picked up a strap wrench and excitedly told his mom about four interesting structures he could make with it. The mom dismissively explained to him why each one was not possible. I did not want to interfere, but I found a couple of his ideas remarkably good. The boy put down the wrench and stopped talking.

The critical faculty is vital — in its place. Edit a paragraph after you write it, not beforehand. Otherwise you will write nothing.

• • •

> When thinking calms down, even a little bit, sound wakes up.
> — William Allaudin Mathieu

In physics the term *relaxation time* refers to the return of a perturbed system to equilibrium. A weight hanging from a string is perturbed by you or me pushing it. Relaxation time is the interval required for the pendulum to stop swinging. If the pendulum is being pushed by you *and* me *and* other people, it will jiggle in many directions and take longer to stop. When a pendulum has finally come to rest, you can choose deliberately to poke it with your finger, imparting a clear, beautiful movement to it. If you poke it too soon, while the pendulum is still perturbed from its previous movements, the result will be random agitation.

In this pendulum we see the connection between effective improvising and contemplative practice, the mind in a meditative state versus the mind in a state of agitation.

Imagine the pendulum swinging, buffeted by forces that

seem to come from the outside. Contemplative practice allows us time for that agitated system to settle down. We begin to listen, to our own voice as well as to outside sounds. Only then can we become active again, and from this calm, produce an improvised gesture. In doing so, we balance two seemingly opposite movements: acting without hesitation and remaining still long enough for perception to dilate and take in the unknown. With evenly hovering attention, we learn that our creative efforts, or our efforts in managing the problems of everyday life, are part of an interconnected system that cannot remain fixed and knowable.

· · ·

Sticking is an activity. We do it, or hold back from doing it. F.M. Alexander discovered, by experimenting on himself, ways to recognize how we stiffen muscles, hold old patterns in place, and limit the good use of our body. He spoke of practicing *inhibition*, that is, recognizing the habit of sticking and choosing not to do it rather than feeling our pains and habits as impediments imposed from the outside. This practice became known as the Alexander Technique. Cultivating physical practices, athletic or artistic, or standing relaxed and alert like those Secret Service agents, we discover muscles that are addicted to perpetual contraction. Involuntary contractions of voluntary muscles represent energy that is wasted rather than focused on what we desire to do. As we sit still on the floor for fifteen minutes, tight leg muscles relax into stretch, becoming longer, softer, more flexible. Thus it is with thoughts, emotions, breath. Thoughts and fears that were tight and worrisome recede. We manifest a steadiness of body and mind that is hard to disrupt. The relaxation response needs time to work. When we do that silent work, our capabilities expand. The natural activity of muscles is variation — holding, moving, keeping still, letting go; alternating rhythms of contract, relax, sustain, release.

Every practice incorporates this component: warming up, tuning up, stretching out, being patient while mind and body quiet down a bit and make room for concerted action and response. Musical practice often begins with playing long, slow tones, simple things, finding and saying hello to your fingertips, hands, shoulders, arms, back, legs, feet, saying hello to sound. Even in everyday conversation, we have these warm-ups: the polite introductions and recitations of formulaic dialogue — hello, how are you, fine — which seem so silly and repetitive to children. Yet people need a period of time to become present to each other through those little rituals.

Thus, some form of meditation, however we conceive of it, is profoundly useful in the practice of any art. Allow that perturbed pendulum to arrive back at the center. Take ordinary, everyday perceptions. Dial their intensity up and down. Visualize a knob, as on an electronic device, at whatever location your right hand currently occupies. Turn the dial up and down on intensity, contrast, tone, color, compression, or expansion of the difference between loud and subtle. Increase and decrease the range of sensitivity. Dial up the spectrum between fine focus and broad view. Dial in sounds or smells, the details of rooms or landscapes, and then dial out again to a larger context. Dial into touch and proprioception. Close your eyes and know where your hand is, and how it is moving. You know how much something weighs by holding it. Dial down the internal dialogue and superfluous brain buzz, like an engineer dialing down the gain, until attention floats lightly. Allow the agitated pendulum to come to rest; then set it gently swinging once more.

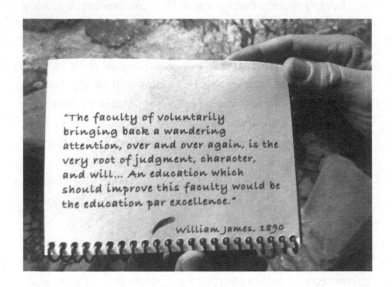

"The faculty of voluntarily bringing back a wandering attention, over and over again, is the very root of judgment, character, and will... An education which should improve this faculty would be the education par excellence."

William James, 1890

Finger-Kissing

To me, "good" is not how skillfully you do something you were taught, but rather discovering something within you in a way that is totally new, unexpected, surprising, and satisfyingly right.
— Rachel Rosenthal

The musician Johann van Beethoven had a talented little boy. A career in the arts was a bit dubious in the 1770s, as it always has been. There were a few superstars, but for most people music was a risky business. The elder Beethoven had in mind the recent successes of another talented child, Mozart, who traveled with his father and sister to dazzle the crowned heads of Europe. Little Ludwig van Beethoven was going to be the goose that laid the golden egg. So the father (in keeping with the pedagogical principles of the time) stood over the boy with a stick as he practiced, and whacked him on the fingers every time he made a mistake. Lest we think this abusive discipline is what made Beethoven a great musician, remember the thousands of just-average musicians who were taught in the same way. Or the thousands who might have enjoyed playing music but quit.

Nowadays we regard it as barbaric to use corporal

punishment as a teaching method. But the shadow of that stick, whacking the child on his or her fingers, remains in other forms. We are taught to fear mistakes and to hide them.

I gave a series of workshops at the Juilliard School in New York, where the students were far more skilled musicians than I will ever be. One afternoon a group of students, who had never previously improvised, progressed from singing some amusing gibberish pieces to picking up their instruments and playing full-on spontaneous music. They played two exquisite improvisations — beautifully organized, emotional pieces. They were connecting with, listening to, and supporting each other. The other musicians, listening in the circle of support, could not believe that these pieces had not been composed. Then the group played a third piece, in which they were a bit out of sync and out of tune with each other. During the discussion following that third piece, the students' faces were drawn with guilt, feeling that they had screwed up. "Mistakes" in improvisation are hard to define, but people recognize when something works and when it doesn't.

The ghost of Beethoven's father was stalking us with his stick, whacking those students on the fingertips for making a mistake. So I thought of prescribing an antidote. I asked them to put their instruments down and do some finger-kissing exercises. They simply walked around the room kissing their own fingers, contemplating and appreciating all ten of them. Finger-kissing is easy. Anyone can do it. In fact, I suggest you try it right now.

A student asked me why I didn't stop the "bad" piece and say something right then. We all have the built-in expectation that a conductor or teacher will wave a baton to offer corrections. Rehearsals and lessons are usually a matter of constant starting and stopping to point out errors. With a large orchestra rehearsing an hour-long Mahler symphony, it's hard to avoid this, though conductors vary widely in the emotional tone of their interjections. But these students, playing brief improvisations in a small group, knew quite well what they liked and didn't like about their piece. It was there in front of everybody's eyes, ears, and minds.

The group went on to play more pieces, which were increasingly strong, varied, and interesting. The more pieces they played, the further away they got from ideas of good and bad. Each piece became its own little world of relationship, information, and feeling. Listening to each other, stepping back from attempting to be individually excellent and pass some imaginary exam, was the key. What they needed at that moment was not assessment; it was mindfulness.

• • •

Finger-kissing is simple, but it rakes up all kinds of wounds. In our own lives, we often betray ourselves by allowing a fixed identity to be attached to us. I have run into many people who were told in the fourth grade that they couldn't carry a tune or who tried to play the piano and were told they were making too many mistakes. They were scolded about these mistakes in a way that stuck to them, that made them want never to touch another instrument again, never to sing again. Or they may wish to sing again, but they believe that they can't, that they lack the fixed, identifiable "quality" of musicality. Some teacher has laid a container around them, laid an identity on them as somebody who isn't musical. Many of us carry similar stories with us, a semipermanent part of our life baggage. The entertainment industries, by pushing highly produced media before our eyes, by emphasizing the importance of superstars, do the same thing. Why try being creative when there is such a gap between what we can do and what is promoted "out there"? We carry many limitations with us, thinking they are part of our identity. If we're lucky, we may later discover that we can step out of that characterization, that the label laid on us does not confine us.

Working together, learning together, is not always a smooth process. We experience interjections, interruptions, awkward silences. As carefully as we might listen to each other, there are places where we blurt out a thought, a feeling, a sound that pushes boundaries, that opens up old or new scars. The engines of guilt — finger-slapping, finger-whacking, finger-pointing — are endemic in our society. In school, in the workplace, we are inundated with assessments and evaluations. These assessments are backed up by threats. Students take standardized tests; teachers in public schools, and the schools themselves, are evaluated by how well their students do on these tests. Probably every student, especially students in the arts and humanities, has experienced the psychological threat of burger flipping — that you may spend the rest of your life doing menial jobs. We fear falling off the treadmill of constant assessment. That mindset doesn't end with school. It pervades much of our society, particularly in the wake of economic recessions, when many of our institutions have been fine-tuned to present an atmosphere of permanent scarcity. And behind all this fear, deeply ingrained in our collective values, is the idea of a God who punishes our transgressions. Students often believe that if they make a mistake it is because they are bad, stupid, or unworthy. This is the cultural background that we're trying to overcome by getting people to open up.

This is the unsettled, uncomfortable aspect of art, of

theater, of teaching. This is the subtext of fear and consequence that underlies students' anxieties and inhibitions, that leads them to conflate their own mistakes with ineptitude — believing that they aren't good enough, that they aren't among the chosen few. We are out on a perilous ledge, working in ways that scrape against the established modes. The discipline of improvising is being comfortable with being uncomfortable.

* * *

One of the finest teachers of improvisational performance I have known is Al Wunder, an old friend from Berkeley who now runs the Theatre of the Ordinary in Melbourne, Australia. Wunder wrote an influential paper called "Positive Feedback Only," reprinted in *The Wonder of Improvisation*. He points us to an experience that many of us have had, being in the room with a one-year-old baby who is walking for the first time:

> When the adults realized what was happening, they all sat in a circle. The young performer teetered and wobbled from the outstretched arms of one adult to another — ooo's, ahs, smiles, cheers and hand claps all around the circle. There was a huge, beaming smile on the child's face. Not a single adult thought of saying, "That was lovely (insert your own name), now if you could just hold your back a little straighter and lift your knees higher, you will walk even better the next time." Why not? The child certainly was not walking well. Yet we, the adults, knew that the child would continue to develop, on their own, the skills of walking, of running, skipping, hopping and other forms of exciting locomotion.

Fine musicians and artists teaching master classes, with the best of intentions, often fall into the trap of making helpful suggestions. It is much more challenging to allow the mistakes to hang silently in the air and instead have the students speak about what they enjoyed in each other's performances. Reinforce what was interesting, and it will be stronger next time. Once a nurturing environment has been established, it is possible to give and receive criticism without wounding. Even then, it is better to use our discernment to find the good, the interesting elements in the work, the edge of exploration that leads to the next work.

What if the dignity and encouragement we show to babies were a model for all our educational systems?

"Positive feedback only," as Wunder describes it, does not mean pretending that everything is uniformly good or that our critical faculty is to be disabled. It means that by searching out the aspects of a performance that we enjoy, we are strengthening them. We can only identify these aspects and figure out how to reinforce them if our brains and perceptions are fully engaged.

In the face of institutional mania for evaluation and the accompanying threats of failure, more positive approaches have also arisen, from the practice of appreciative inquiry in the world of business and organizational consulting, which has spread widely from its origins in the Cleveland School of Business, to some of the methods of legendary basketball coach Phil Jackson (who introduced his players to Zen meditation and mindfulness techniques as part of his training regime) and his Positive Coaching Alliance, an antidote to the popular conception of sports coaches as militaristic, punishing martinets.

• • •

At this moment you might be sitting, standing, lying down, or walking. Wherever you are, try gently shifting from side to side. If you're sitting, notice that as your torso keels a bit to the right, the muscles on your left side *know* to pull you back to the left to return upright. Every time you veer over to the left, your muscles adjust you back to the right. We do this every moment of the day; otherwise, we wouldn't be sitting up in chairs, we'd be flopped onto the floor like corpses. Our proprioceptive senses and core muscles are in a constant dance of dynamic equilibrium. We perceive where our bodies are, we perceive our relationships with the people and objects around us, and we adjust accordingly.

In the same way, we are able to walk, bicycle, drive a car, dance. This is the wisdom of the self-adjusting body. Steering a car, we continually guide it right and left in order to go straight. We do not castigate ourselves for making a mistake each time we wiggle the wheel. We simply notice the error and adjust for it. Inevitably we will lose our balance, fall over, make mistakes, and get into accidents. How do we respond? With guilt and self-punishment? Or with self-acceptance, which encourages another attempt and more practice, allowing us to respond to emergencies smoothly and realistically? Self-correction is a lot easier without the added burden of guilt.

Wunder reminds us that when toddlers fall, they don't need to be told that they fell. We trust that they know what is happening as it happens, that they receive feedback as the experience unfolds. Our bodies and minds, our partnerships with others, are self-organizing systems. The mechanisms of feedback, communication, self-correction, self-organization, by which toddling evolves into graceful interaction, are fundamental to life, as revealed in the sciences of systems theory.

Every person reading this is an ex-toddler. We retain (consciously or unconsciously) an immense amount of experience from this life stage of falldown-getup, falldown-getup, falldown-getup. Nelson Mandela once said that he wanted to be judged not by what he accomplished but by how many times he fell down and got up again.

Improvising is trial and error smoothly flowing. For that to work, error has to be free from clenching or regret, so that our learning process can swing easily from each step to the next. The more we accept mistakes as part of the natural flow of our activity, the more we will be able to incorporate them, use them to build stronger and more interesting structures. In the flow of music, the "bad" note can be deliberately repeated, now as a bridge to something new, building a new modulation around it. Our partners can pick it up and toss it around in a freshly expanded game.

•   •   •

Shunryū Suzuki, following the thirteenth-century Zen master Dōgen, said that life is "one continuous mistake." Miles Davis said, "Do not fear mistakes, there are none." They were both saying the same thing. One continuous mistake means continuous evolution. We never stop toddling.

Suzuki-roshi also proposed that the best way to control a horse is to give it a large pasture and simply observe it. Mindfulness is the key, not control in the sense of grabbing someone and making them do something.

I like the French meaning of the word for *control*, the verb *controller*, which isn't about forcing people to do as you wish but rather investigating the status of things. A conductor on a train is said to *controller les billets* — check to see that people have tickets. Yes, he can throw you off the train if you don't have a ticket, but *controller* in this context primarily means to pay attention to, to take account of.

Controller might be translated not as "controlling" but as "noticing." Notice without guilt or judgment that a muscle is unnecessarily tense, that our breath is unnecessarily constricted, that a thought is unnecessarily obsessive. Notice that our way of sliding up the instrument's fingerboard involves unnecessary gripping that might result in a jagged sound. Notice that we can deliberately make that jagged sound if we want to. Notice habits in our professional lives or relationships that are the equivalent of these unnecessary body tensions. With heightened attention, we can let go of these tensions as they arise — but without punishing ourselves.

B.F. Skinner, the influential learning theorist, said that the purpose of psychology was "the prediction and control of behavior." This unfortunate worldview was the perfect extension into mid-twentieth-century thought of *both* materialistic, reductionist science *and* controlling, judgmental religion, in which life is shaped by reward and punishment. Think of William Blake's Nobodaddy, the domineering, patriarchal sky-god laying out the rules of the universe with his compasses and punishing his creatures for crossing those boundaries. The idea of reward and punishment is deeply ingrained in our culture, as it is in many others. It is bound up with ideas of power, and the frustration that we cannot control others "for their own good."

To return to Wunder's story of the first-time toddler: the

adults who sit around applauding and cheering are not engaging in some slaphappy delusion that the child is walking perfectly. The child knows when he or she stumbles and falls; the adults know too. They are — *en controllant* — noticing everything.

In other life situations, we don't feel like cheering, and it can be hard work to resist making a biting, judgmental remark. It takes discipline and forbearance to allow the child or student the room to falldown-getup. We may find ourselves mentally reaching for Papa Beethoven's stick. Learning to use the mindfulness of *controller* takes more patience and practice than learning to walk as a baby. And unfortunately, in our twenty-first-century world, there are still some who literally reach for the stick.

Kissing your fingers is a radical, transformative practice. It is not pretense that everything is good or that our mistakes don't matter. They do matter. Finger-kissing is rather a celebration of our personal participation in the immense moment-to-moment labor of learning and evolution.

• • •

Are there mistakes in improvisation? As we get older, we accumulate regrets that we might have said or done *this*, we ought not have said or done *that*. We all have experienced what in Yiddish is called *trepverter* and in French *l'esprit de l'escalier*, that moment when we have just had an unsatisfactory conversation with someone; now we're walking down the stairs and realize that if we had only said *x*, the interaction would have gone so much better. We could spend ourselves in remorse (which means "rebiting"), or we can do the deep practice of finger-kissing, which is self-forgiveness. Instead of oscillating between punishment and perfectionism, we can accept falldown-getup as the modus operandi of living as a human being. We can access self-respect and trust in the process — and we can access respect for others, including their mistakes.

The question is often asked, "Can improvisation be taught?" People ask this with a fairly clear understanding that the question itself is a paradox. As soon as you teach, in the sense of transmitting information and methods, you are limiting improvisation. Information and methods are important, but they come in at a different level of learning. The only way to enable improvisation is to step back to create an empty space (and at first, a safe space) into which the participants can move of their own free will. To guide improvisation means giving people permission to do what they already know how to do, opening up a space in which it feels safe to take risks.

Paradoxes are inherent in the teaching of any subject, but improvising brings them to the fore. If I teach students to play in my style, using my methods, then they are not improvising. The balancing act of tradition and originality is something that each person needs to figure out for him- or herself, and it changes throughout our lifetimes. When we present facts and ideas, techniques, histories, and memories, these are doors to the students' own self-organizing systems in progress, not methods or recipes. In teaching, we are, in Blake's words, "striving with systems to deliver individuals from those systems."

• • •

The concept of negative space is vital not only in arts like sculpture or music but also in the art of teaching. I remember catching hell from Gregory Bateson one day, after class, when I was his teaching assistant. A few minutes earlier, I had been displaying my knowledge to the students. "You monkey!" he splurted at me, "I had a nice juicy silence cooking away in there, and you had to stick your big feet in and muck it up!" His gift was patiently developing the organic wholeness of a group, as emergent ideas sprouted from students' interactions — ideas that were both more complex and more integrated with experience than anything that might emerge from a set syllabus. This kind of patience involves stepping back and allowing things to happen in the group. Teachers feel pressured to say something, to come up with activities, when silence can do its work. But we often feel that we don't have time for silence.

Bateson's message about silence in teaching is to allow complex ideas and interactions to take the time they need to cook. Don't take them out of the oven too soon. Don't summarize or package them. Bateson's type of teaching takes more time and patience than handing out prepackaged units of curriculum.

As I have grown older I have learned to teach by saying less and less. Body movements, gestures, nods, eye movements — inviting people to contribute their expressions, ideas, images, without saying much; occasionally without even asking questions; letting silence and movement become the questions. "What do you want us to do?" My hands toss the question back where it belongs, and people always step up and do something. The less I prescribe, the more interesting the something is. These movements are part of the repertoire of conducting. We think of conducting as communicating the emotional and structural tone of a written musical score, but the unwritten yet definite patterns that people have to contribute are just as much part of the score.

Even when the context is standing up and giving a talk onstage, some of the talks that have given me the most satisfaction (and some of the most satisfying talks I have heard others give), are those in a foreign environment where a translator is needed. If the talk lasts an hour, you simply can't talk for more than half an hour. If I say half as many words, they are often twice as good.

This type of minimalist teaching is not quite the same as Socratic teaching, but the two are closely related. Socratic teaching is also called maieutics (spiritual midwifery) — leading the students down a path with open-ended questions, allowing space for them to come to conclusions on their own. This is not a matter (as in Plato's *Meno* dialogue) of letting students come on their own to a conclusion that we could have told them, but rather leading to a conclusion that we could *not* have told them, that only *they* could have arrived at.

My job as a teacher is not to lead, but to nurture, and to encourage students to have the gumption to do what is theirs to do. Maintaining a nurturing environment in which people feel safe to explore and experiment: that is the essence of education. We try to fill up empty space and time, afraid to let them stay empty. This is partly because of our own natural nervousness. Also, if one is a public speaker, a teacher, a consultant, a counselor, a performer, or any number of other professions, one feels that one has to give people their money's worth. That puts pressure on us to fill our time with activity rather than standing back and allowing things to mature. Sometimes it takes a colossal output of energy to remain calmly quiet and not intervene.

Stepping back and creating space is the very marrow of this work: it's not just about how to teach improv in a class but about how we teach ourselves, as individuals and as partners in relationships, how to be human beings.

Thirty-five years after Bateson told me that I was talking too much, I experienced what was for me the ultimate reward. It came at the conclusion of a four-day residency at a university with students and faculty from a mixture of departments, from music education to philosophy to engineering. At the end of the final evening, eighty of us were up on a round stage. An evening of improvising and discussion had concluded. The appropriate thing for me to do was to step forward and thank my hosts for their magnanimity and their beautiful job of organizing the events of the past days; thank the participants for their imaginative, skillful, and brave contributions; wish everyone farewell; and express the hope that we stay in touch. But something possessed me to say nothing. Standing at the edge of the circle of participants, I took a couple of steps backward, and again said nothing. Two minutes of silence ticked away. Then one professor lifted up a foot and tapped it, then again and again. Someone else joined in on the rhythm, slapping her shoulders in syncopation; someone else pulled up her cello and played another layer of sound. The foot tapping, body-slapping, singing, and finger-snapping spread around the circle until all eighty bodies were involved. Then the dance began.

• • •

An afternoon in Argentina. Young musicians circled up. Each in turn declaimed a solo, with instrument or voice or movement, or all three. Each took his or her sweet time to step up out of the stillness; it was a bit like a Quaker meeting. The next person who had something to say rose up from the nourishing sea of silence and played her heart out on her saxophone, wild. She finished, with a look of incredible dignity on her face as she sat. Then another person rose. The diversity of styles and personalities was fascinating, but what united the musicians was this sense of dignity. They were not worried about being better or worse than Bach, Stravinsky, Coltrane, Shankar, Dylan, Piazzolla. The seriousness on their faces was that of children in deep play, filled with concentration, clarity, and intensity, as each made a distinctive statement in sound, then stepped back into the collective stillness. The statements were not merely sound; they were the multimodal expression of the human body, face, voice, mind in movement. The solos fed the group, and the group fed the solos.

As I watched these young men and women play with such originality and integrity, a phrase from the Italian Renaissance popped into my mind. Giannozzo Manetti (1452) and Pico della Mirandola (1486) both wrote influential orations called "On the Dignity and Excellence of Man." (They forgot to mention Woman, but today we can fix that.) Such ideas were revolutionary then, marked by people beginning to think for themselves, be themselves, discover artistic and scientific truth by experience and experiment rather than trying to make experience square with the dogma of clerics and kings. The dignity and excellence of human beings, the power of free expression and learning, was promulgated by people who often risked and sometimes lost their lives. And these struggles of art and science against the clerics and kings of the world are far from over. This is the motif that came to me as I watched these students play for each other. How wonderful people are that they can do this, make bold and exquisite art with clarity and simplicity, and connect directly with other human beings. They can speak for themselves and with each other in their own fresh language.

Finger-kissing sprouted as a humorous way to exorcise an old musical ghost. But it is more. It makes visible the gifts of improvised living: joy, trust, self-respect, and mutual respect. These are better, and more supportive of life, than mere perfection.

•

This Moment

A continuous present is a continuous present.
— Gertrude Stein

I love the instant theater of playing music that feels just right for now and then disappears forever. I also love how good it feels to delete a sentence from a paragraph I wrote twenty years ago. That sentence and its neighbors had always bothered me. I tried to fix them from time to time but never managed. Then I simply deleted it, and now the neighbors are happy and the paragraph moves unimpeded. Hitting the delete key takes place in an instant, but getting to the point of hitting it has taken a long time.

The ancient Greeks spoke of two kinds of time, or two experiences of time: *chronos* and *kairos*. *Chronos* is what we now call clock time, objective time. In music, *chronos* is metronome time. *Kairos* is timeliness, the opportune moment that surges out from our experience, something that cannot happen at any time but only at *this* time. Educators call it the teachable moment. Hitting the delete key on that sentence takes place in the enhanced reality of *kairos*. In *chronos* it takes either half a second or twenty years.

There is a saying from the sixteenth-century Japanese tea master Sen no Rikyū: *ichi-go ichi-e*. Literally it means "one time, one meeting." A once-in-a-lifetime encounter, unprecedented and unrepeatable. Tea ceremony is a highly ritualized activity; at first glance it seems far from improvisational. Practitioners can spend a lifetime perfecting their skills handling utensils, creating the ambience of the space, refining the very formal decorum of their interaction with participants. The host and guest interact in a strictly prescribed sequence: you sit just so, the water is poured just so, the tea whisk is handled just so. The guest raises the bowl slightly and then turns it to drink from the rear edge to express humility and appreciation, and both participants understand the significance that codifies. Beginning, middle, and end are defined, and the same host and guests may enact a tea ceremony in the future. But today's experience can never be reproduced: the call of a wild bird outside mixing with the sound of the kettle at boiling point, the conversation at different points picking up, slowing down, and lapsing into quiet, the deliberate nature of each gesture combining and blending with the unforeseen environmental factors of light and sound form a permeable whole that allows for both experiences of time, *chronos* and *kairos*. The result is that this meticulous ritual becomes a context for the participants to deeply realize the impermanence and preciousness of their interaction *just now*.

In this sense, *chado*, the "Way of Tea," is not unlike many concerts of Western classical music. A concert is a ritualized form of social interaction and specialized craft. Though a piece may be performed repeatedly with the same or similar parameters, every time it is a unique experience, in one way or another. The point of undertaking the ritual is that despite its highly structured and precise nature, it is an encounter that cannot be predicted, controlled, or re-created.

In this moment, preparing and creating, the technical and the sacred, flow together seamlessly like a devotional dance. And then the moment vanishes. We treat a fleeting encounter with the seriousness of deep play. Our meeting is one of a kind in the history of the universe. It will never be like this again.

Universal Language

When we hear the trill of the thrush in the
flowers, or the voice of the frog in the waters,
we know that every living being has its song.
— Ki no Tsurayuki, 905 CE

When I was about ten years old, I sat on a stool next to the stove while my mother cooked dinner and talked with me about life. She was a Depression-era high school dropout but read everything from Spinoza to the Gnostic Gospels to Virginia Woolf, and mused about them while cooking and cleaning. Her feeling for philosophy went hand in hand with her habit of kissing trees on her walks when she thought no one was looking. That afternoon in the kitchen she turned to me, lifted her right forefinger, paused, and said, "Ubombo!"

We have to start somewhere. When teaching a workshop, I find it wonderful to start with gibberish. *Gibberish*, as I am using it here, is not nonsense, nor is it a cipher for something else; it is vocalization that comes out as pure syllables of sound, not tied to a particular meaning but articulating mood and feeling. It is simple yet capable of carrying a rich depth of expression: a talent that is universal because each of us has been a baby. Everyone can make sound, everyone can move, and everyone has the perceptual finesse to create structured, integrated, and refined improvisational works in collaboration with others.

I always begin a workshop in a circle of support. The first person passes sound and movement to the next, and on to the next, with no gaps, like nerve impulses, no time to question right and wrong. Synapses fire. Sound and movement co-arise together, as a single, simple action. If the sound is laughter (say you crack up at the behavior of the person next to you, or you're nervously giggling), then *that* is your sound. This is not the world of philosophical logic with its true and false propositions. Singing, grunting, shouting, squeaking, humming, writhing, whispering — and pregnant silence — are neither true nor false.

If you are flummoxed, and what comes out is *huh?*, that is the perfectly suitable song emerging, as full of possibilities as any. Indeed, *huh* is the most universal word among the world's languages, more so even than *mama*.

We might pass sound from person to person, beginning with the softest pianissimo and the smallest gesture, an intimate message, and let it build from person to person until it grows into a massive fortissimo bellow. A tiny hand movement expands to earthshaking whole-body exuberance. Or vice versa: we enact a diminuendo from brash to infinitesimal.

What happens when the impulse passes from one person to the next? Instantly, patterns of relationship come into existence. Imitation. Call-and-response. Overlapping contrasts. Exaggerating what the last person did. Plays on relationships like dominance-submission, or symmetrical rivalry, or compromise-peacemaking. Our play is made of abstract sound and movement but contains universal stories. This simple method of making sound and movement together breaks down barriers of language and culture, differences of age and professional identification. It allows people to communicate as equals, with equal measures of profundity and fun. The stakes are low since there is nothing to prove, nothing to gain or lose. Yet the interactivity takes on a musical structure. In the protected context of a workshop, we are allowed to sound or look foolish. There is no pressure to do well. Musicians might transition from making noise back to playing their instruments, seamlessly continuing the conversation in more complex forms of interplay. Actors, singers, and dancers might resume using their bodies in their artful, expert ways. When the participants return to their accustomed forms, they are more sensitive to each other, freer in their experimentation and collaboration. Brain, body, voice, breath, hands, feet, objects — all one song.

• • •

Voice and body are the oldest toys. In an age of high technology, they remain the ultimate toys. Artistic experience that seems frivolous may also allow people entry into a state of being profoundly present with each other and themselves.

As babies we babbled fluently — a continual riot of improvising in an ever-expanding vocabulary of noise and action — playing, complaining, commenting on everything, not hesitating to laugh or cry. We erupted with a huge range of phonemes and tonemes, nearly every sound of every language on earth. Gibberish is the primordial language, which we then whittle down until it begins to match what those around us respond to. All the sounds of all the languages are liable to make an appearance: Xhosa click-talk, French nasals, southern drawl, Chinese tonal shapes. Both my sons as babies and toddlers were adept at the French rolled *R* at the back of their throats, extended for a long time. They could not do this at a later age.

You can have a more meaningful two-way conversation with a baby in gibberish, empty of ordinary signification but full of affective content, than you can in any standard language. As we communicate back and forth with preverbal babies, we learn a great deal about mindfulness and the constantly changing colors of attention. We connect in a direct modality of raw emotion, raw pleasure, raw inquisitiveness.

This experience we all have had as babies qualifies us to improvise today, with the tools and skills we have available to us as adults.

• • •

When I was a boy our family belonged to a conservative synagogue in Los Angeles. They held their services mostly in Hebrew. Hebrew was felt to be a sacred language, the sounds themselves significant, even if you didn't understand them. My parents' generation learned to "read" the Hebrew letters and words, to pronounce and intone the prayers in the book at high speed, without ever learning what the words meant.

I remember wandering up and down the aisles in my uncomfortable suit and tie, surrounded by men and women davening: swaying and bobbing while praying in a language that few in the room understood. To most, it may as well have been gibberish. I thought this was ridiculous. Either (I muttered at the grownups under my breath) learn the language so you know what you are saying, or pray in English. That fit with many of my feelings about established religion, about people blindly conforming to formulaic behavior. Then I escaped with a group of other bored kids to the tropical fish store next door.

Many years later, after I had become an improvisational violinist, I came to realize that growing up with all that mysterious chanting around me was a vital root of my work. I had been exposed, year after year, to the sight and sound of men and women swaying, muttering, and singing syllables with heartfelt emotion, with a distinct understated musicality — and with the feeling that what they were saying was the most important thing in the world. It was the sound. The lexical meaning of words is all right as far as it goes, but it is the sound that can affect us with equal or even greater power to reflect emotion, pattern, and purpose.

Still later, at age thirty, I found myself sitting in the wee hours of the morning at San Francisco Zen Center, intoning the Heart Sutra in Japanese, a language I don't know. There I was, doing exactly what I had made fun of as a child. Of course, the texts are inherently significant as philosophy and poetry. In all such languages — Hebrew, Japanese, Tibetan, Sanskrit, Latin, Arabic, Yoruba, and many others — the deep practitioners know the layers of language intimately, and the history behind the words matters. Still, there is something about pure sound, as mantra, something irreducibly beautiful about surrendering to its waves.

•　•　•

I have long come to think of the violin and bow as a kind of polygraph machine for the heart — truth detector, lie detector, registering minute vibrations of muscle and nerve, revealing a subconscious world of information and feeling. So it is for the vocal chords and breath, all the tones and noises we make, revealing subtle patterns that cannot be expressed in mere words.

•   •   •

The most important example of musical gibberish as self-expressive art is, of course, scat. Scat in jazz was sometimes credited to Louis Armstrong, when he stepped up to the microphone and forgot the words to either "I'm a Ding Dong Daddy" or "Heebie Jeebies," though we know that Gene Greene and other artists preceded him. Scat's history in recordings by African American musicians is long and storied — brought to flower by Ella Fitzgerald, the great Sarah Vaughan, and many others. Likewise, in Indian music there is a long history of expressive syllabary, drumming with the voice, and raga singing. The almost infinite variety of breath sounds, with or without electronic modification, can provide a lifetime of fruitful experimentation. Songs without words. Breathing into a microphone. Beatboxing. Speech play. Sound poetry. *Spielsprache. Sprechstimme*. The uninhibited yells of men and women in martial arts practice. *Katzu!* Syllables — those most everyday beautiful things that we all carry in our mouths — are among the wonders of the world. And with all the variations of tone and expression, there are millions of them. Then we get into the vast intermediate territory between breath, speech, singing, groaning, laughter.

The Bible claims that the universe began in a stochastic muddle called *tohu-bohu* — a euphonic name quite different in tone from its English translation, "without form and void." From the *tohu-bohu* of supposed randomness, patterns cohere, evolution begins, and life takes on its distinctive shapes.

• • •

We usually think of language as a collection of symbols, something that stands for something else. But language floats in a sea of paralanguage — all that is carried above, beyond, underneath, and around the words we speak. Body language, tone, people talking at a higher pitch when they are lying or defensive; lower, softer, and slower when they are comfortable.

By eliminating language, gibberish gets us into the underlying texture of paralanguage and metacommunication: creating relationship through affective tone. It is analog, not digital. *Analog* means continuously variable, the way your finger can slide freely up the strings of a violin; *digital* means discrete or discontinuous like the keys on a piano. The analog elements of language cannot be codified by the alphabet and lexical meaning; they classify, contextualize, and connect. The letters of the alphabet are digital coding: there is no letter that slides halfway between A and B. But the way I say *A* is analog and fluid, carrying mood in tone and timing. The ways in which I might widen my eyes while saying *mood* are infinitely variable.

When we play music, we are deep beneath the sea of paralanguage, where sounds don't have strict meanings; yet they are eloquent, intense, and in some cases incommunicable through ordinary means. This makes it sound as though music is purely analog. However, in reality, like life itself, music is compounded of analog and digital elements, depending on your vantage point, much like the simultaneous existence of light as wave and particle. Jazz and blues musicians are trained to improvise over "the changes," meaning the change of an underlying chord, let's say from A7 to D9.

But the first principle of life is that *everything* changes. Every millisecond, and in every direction, we are surrounded by changes, and often the changes come not in abrupt binary switches but in gradient spectral shifts, slowly morphing, with the infinite variability of widened eyes. Can we play life's changes, transitioning between phases as smoothly as the blackbird swoops down to land on a scraggy field in a seamless arc, or the infant boy as he rolls his *R*s from a high pitch down to a low growl?

• • •

One day I said something about signs to my friend Rebekah. In the middle of my sentence, she asked, "Signs? ↗" with an upward swoop to the pitch of her voice. I replied, "Signs, as opposed to symbols." Two kinds of communication. A sign is a symptom that is inherent to an activity, as thunder is a sign of a storm or a blush is a sign of embarrassment. A symbol is deliberate, a packet of information that "stands for" something else. Then she said, "Oh ↘ ..." — her pitch swinging back down to its resting place. As she intoned "Signs?" with a lifting lilt, her head tilted up. Her head remained high during the pause, eyes expectant. Then her head dropped along with her pitch as she said "Oh." The three phases were of equal duration — a rhythm. That was a pretty and melodic song, in which voice and body movement were not separate.

"Signs? ↗"   {pause}   "Oh ↘ ..."

The movement of those tones created, in miniature, the classic musical or dramatic structure of tension and resolution. Communication is the external sign of an interior pattern of being, as in our image of the musical instrument as a polygraph of the heart. The Anglican Book of Common Prayer defines a sacrament as "an outward and visible sign of an inward and spiritual grace." Rebekah was making these sounds *while* I was talking. Theoretically, in conversation, people take turns and speak sequentially, exchanging bits of information, whereas in music they can play simultaneously, in counterpoint. In practice, these distinctions fall away.

• • •

The great medieval composer, mystic, and abbess, Saint Hildegard of Bingen (1098–1179), invented a language called Lingua Ignota. There is all manner of speculation as to its purpose: Was it for secret rituals and mystical rites, or for covert communication? Because she was a saint, no one seems to consider the possibility that she was having fun, sufficient unto itself. As I typed the previous sentence, I almost wrote "that she was *just* having fun." The *just* is an automatism or cliché that means "merely," as though fun would be more important if it had a purpose, were a means to an end. Thus the utilitarian biases of our society. As Westerners we're culturally trained to ask the question, "Why?" — always looking for a purpose or a reason behind things. It's a peculiar obsession that prevents us from letting a thing, an event, an experience, an emotion, an action exist for what it is. Inherently complete.

Similar speculations about serious religious, magical, or educational purpose are projected all the way back to prehistoric art, like the cave paintings at Lascaux and Chauvet. Perhaps the creators of that art were also having fun with line and color, hand and eye; and perhaps, most important, there is no sharp dividing line, no need to choose between religious awe and the pleasure of play. Likewise, with overly simplified popular ideas of evolutionary biology, we love to impute purpose. If it's not for the serious matter of species survival, if it doesn't have a "point," why should it exist? Thus the sociobiology fad in which we have to explain every element of animal or human life as directly serving some survival need, projecting our limited idea of "economic man" on the rest of the living universe.

. . .

In a semi-darkened theater in Seattle, five players stand onstage. I hold up a Rorschach inkblot card. One person (an Austrian actor) turns to the other players and says *chuchaki* in a stage whisper. From that seed arises a fifteen-minute piece of theater. It consists of three acts: a quintet, a duo, and a quintet. *Chuchaki* passes from person to person, sometimes in a guilty whisper, sometimes in the lyrical form of a Gregorian chant, sometimes in an exultant shout, a march, along with many other sounds. People appear, hiding in the wings, popping out again in sculptural formations of bodies. A

woman breaks off at one point as a rhythm section, kneeling, rubbing her jeans to make scrubbing sounds as the audience joins in with rhythmic finger snaps. She grunts exuberantly: *Chuchaki! Chuchaki!* It is beautiful, hilarious, sacred.

Three years later, some of the same players meet again in a workshop in Berlin. A woman says wistfully, "I wish we could do another piece like that one about the beach." Puzzlement from the others: "What one about the beach?" "Chuchaki." "Oh, you mean the one about death!" One person thinks it was about the beach, another thinks it was about death, another thinks it was about her parents. I think *chuchaki* is baby talk that has no fixed meaning, invented on the spot by participants in a theater workshop I taught, and that I remember because it sounds so delicious to sing. Dead people, people enjoying a beach, or a family arguing in a house — the "about" doesn't matter; it was an immersion in shifting relationships of people in movement, patterns of interaction. Before meaning, language is music. Like instrumental music, it has a tone, a shape, a dynamic. You can't pin it down or define it, but you can feel it and be moved into your own deep awareness.

But today, writing this, I decided to approach the shrine of St. Google, and discovered that *chuchaqui* is a real word in Ecuadorean (the Andean Quechua language) for a hangover. Ubombo.

·

Bedtime Stories

> *Return again to the rhythmic recitations that are*
> *so familiar to us, so familiar that we know them*
> *by heart even in a translation two or three times*
> *removed: admirable Aramaic images repeated,*
> *while descending the Mount, by those privileged*
> *listeners to the Sermon of the divine Improviser.*
> — Marcel Jousse,
> *Le Style oral rythmique*

Once upon a time, when my sons were little, they demanded that I tell them bedtime stories. They especially liked stories about Odysseus, or James Bond, or best of all, stories that combined Odysseus and James Bond. The stories had to balance set pieces and surprises. I was expected to know how much old material to repeat and how much new to invent. Night after night these stories began with the same invocation:

Once upon a time there were three little pigs, a momma pig, a poppa pig, and a little pink baby pig. The three pigs were cared for by the kindly old swineherd, Eumaeus. Eumaeus lived in a hut and worked for his friend Odysseus, who was far away on the ocean. Odysseus put on his armor and bows and arrows and sailed far away to fight the Trojans.

But then the nightly stories diverged. Odysseus was here, he was there, he was tricking a one-eyed giant who wanted to eat him, he was back home in disguise. His friend James Bond had to appear out of nowhere, little green sports car roaring down the beach of Ithaca, scattering the suitors. Or James Bond was disguised as a good-for-nothing Greek gambler playing cards and drinking in Penelope's hall, the better to spy on the villains. James Bond and Odysseus had to rescue each other from dire straits, but where and how had to be different every time.

Bedtime stories. Sometimes we read them from a book, sometimes we make them up on the spot, sometimes it's half and half. The words are a little different each night, but the gist of the story recurs in eternal variation. Children enjoy surprise and repetition in equal measure. They might remind us in our improvisational storytelling: Mom, Dad, you forgot to tell the part about the blind man who could see the future. Oh yes, we admit, and tell that part. On some nights omissions and mistakes are not that important; they get swallowed up in the action. On some nights the children demand precision.

• • •

Homer, whoever he or she was, improvised the *Odyssey*. We used to wonder where that thrilling poetry came from. Homer epitomized our rock-solid idea of classics, enshrined in written notation. It was assumed for ages that the great epic tales, though orally transmitted for generations until they were written down, were essentially *texts* that were meticulously composed by someone and then memorized. There may have been changes along the way, but these were errors of transmission. But how could the Homeric epics remain so beautiful and fresh after so many centuries? Did the ancient bards have such prodigious and exact memories as to faithfully reproduce the poetry of one long-gone primordial genius? And there are many other vast ancient poems, such as the Norse Eddas, or India's *Ramayana* and the *Mahabharata*, which is thirteen times longer than the Bible — all these masterpieces presumably the work of unfathomably great ancient bards.

In the 1920s and '30s a young American scholar, Milman Parry, revolutionized literary studies. He put together linguistic evidence that the structure of Homer's epics is not consistent with written composition but rather with spoken-word improvisation created out of formulaic phrases and recycled story parts. These works were composition-in-performance, assembled in real time in the rap of rhythmic speech, enabled by the musical movement of cyclic patterns. Writers used to refer to the ancient bards (or the Muse) as *singing*, yet that term wasn't taken literally enough. Oral transmission is based not on verbatim memory but on active re-creation. Stock phrases, and elements of well-known mythology, are recombined into new sequences, all fitting into steadily rolling rhythms. Homer's poetry is full of epithets for wine, for the sea, for the many gods and people in the stories. The epithets have varying numbers of syllables and beats; the storyteller could pluck one or another so that they would fall together like Tetris pieces to fit the six-beat line, the basic shape of the ongoing poem. Phrases are flung into place in the act of telling, fitting into the metrical and musical passage.

Parry's breakthrough was to look for clues to "the Homeric question" not only in the fossil record of texts but also in the artistic practices of present-day people with traditions of unwritten long-form poetic improvisation. This was not unlike the meticulous work of Darwin, who sought corroborating signs of ongoing evolution in contemporary animals. Scholars whom Parry met in Paris, Marcel Jousse and Matthias Murko, put him on to the presence of living illiterate epic singers in the Balkans who moved from town to town singing stories of past battles, re-creating the story fresh each time — yet each time confident they were telling "the" story. To gather evidence, Parry carted phonograph equipment to what was then the Kingdom of Yugoslavia to record the bards of Bosnia. Here were the remote, mountainous places north of Greece where Odysseus was told (his penance to propitiate Poseidon) to carry an oar until he met men who had never seen the sea, who thought the oar was a winnowing fan. The epics retold folkloric tales from local history, old battles between Turks and Europeans, but each time the stories were told anew for social gatherings large and small. The plotlines were well known. Reusing combinations and permutations of formulaic language allowed skilled singers to keep the rhythmic poetry flowing for hours or days at a time.

Parry and his student Albert Lord, followed by others, went into the field and richly documented this oral poetic tradition. Their detective work lay in comparing the millennia-old Homeric verses with the live improvisations of the present day, and seeing, though the stories and the poetic forms were different, that they shared the same types of pattern language — shaped differently from composed texts.

After Parry's death from a stupid gun accident in Los Angeles in 1935, Albert Lord extended and expanded his work into *The Singer of Tales* (1960). A long line of scholars deepened the inquiry into improvised oral poetry, long epics and short lyrics, and found it all over the world, in cultures with and without literary traditions. Many European tales, thought to be texts whose sources were lost in medieval times, are part of this canvas of oral creativity: *Beowulf*, the *chansons de geste*, the *Song of the Nibelungen*. Soon we learned that these traditions were nearly universal throughout Africa, Asia, the Americas, and Oceania. Improvisatory poets who sing for hire in Sardinia are among the many forms of spoken-word expression — invention combined with tradition — that have persisted through the centuries. Elsewhere, bards, troubadours, minstrels, jongleurs. The universe of oral-rhythmic improv includes West African griots keeping alive ancient genealogies and Tibetan singers weaving new songs of Milarepa and re-creating the heroic and farcical exploits of King Gesar of Ling. In Japan the *biwa hōshi* would re-create old feudal epics of bloody battles and political karma.

Poetic singers accompany themselves on string instruments, bowed or plucked. In medieval France, *chansons de geste* were sung along with the *vielle*, an ancestor of the violin. In Japan, the lute-like *biwa*. In the Delta blues, the guitar. The Bosnian bards studied by Parry accompanied themselves on a *guslé*, a one-string fiddle that harkens back to the ancient Greek tradition of lyre and cithara players. They were using music, and particularly stringed instruments, to construct and perform immense, complex stories, many of which have been transcribed into text and stand as admired and beloved literary achievements millennia later.

Parry's and Lord's original work suggested that there were two immiscible modes of culture, *orality* and *literacy*. It seemed that where one ends the other begins. But that dichotomy is long gone. Oral literature is not a practice only of tribal societies untouched by modernity; oral poets abound in the modern technological world and can often swing between writing work down and making it up on the spot with voice and body. For example, with the *bertso* form in Basque country, contestants sing about romance or soccer, competing in the Bertso Derby — judged tournaments of improvised poetry reminiscent of Keith Johnstone's Theatre-Sports — in front of big audiences in urban auditoriums. Cell phone technicians moonlight as improvisational poets.

Our modern ears hear *improvising* as creating something all new and of this moment. It might seem contradictory to improvise with prefabricated materials: epithets, formulas, well-known story lines. We like to think of creativity as fresh and new. But it is possible to be fresh and old. Artists like Homer were called *rhapsodes*, from the Greek words for *stitching* and *singing*: to *rhapsodize* means to stitch a song together.

When I imagine Homer telling his or her oral epics, bedtime stories are my paradigm. The plot keeps reassembling itself to more or less the same shape, the favorite phrases and epithets get reused night after night, but always in a different way.

· · ·

And then there are the repeated, re-improvised epics that sadly we keep acting out as real history. Go back to those Balkan tales that Parry and Lord studied: recombinant sagas of Muslims jostling against Christians on the fluid borderlands of Europe and Asia Minor. South Slavic against North Muslim. Greeks against Turks. Christians against Ottomans. Keep on going back, to the Crusades. And before that the Greeks against the Trojans. Go forward, to the battles of the Middle East in the twenty-first century. The slaughter goes on, from Homer's time to ours. And like poetry and drama, the actual history is made of formulas, clichés, the same old stories and myths being dressed up again in different costumes. All presented as unfolding news: new, new news, except that it is a retelling of a story from ancient times.

·   ·   ·

We find a similar blending of convention and invention in the genesis of jazz. The Homeric epics were composed in performance much as traditional jazz is improvised: a kit of ingredients — tunes, chord progressions, and rhythms, shaken together into a fresh utterance, variations on well-known standard tunes that we have heard a thousand times before but never this way, never before in this personal style. The jazz standards are analogous to the bards' often-repeated myths, and the chord changes, the harmonic forms and twists, are analogous to the epithets and verbal formulas. When these items are put together by an individual artist or a commingling group, the result can emerge as a live, unbroken experience that is fresh and of the moment. We are playing on the continuum between free improv and replication of a known pattern. A jazz musician picks a standard tune, Erroll Garner's "Misty," dancing around the latticework of the tune's harmonic structure. She may work through chord changes, melodic embellishment, or climb around the structure of a preexisting mode or scale. The dance steps are new, the latticework is old. Jazz is neither free improvisation, nor a faithful hewing to tradition, but a hybrid of the two. Speaking with the form and giving it a new voice.

In spontaneous art, the moment of performance and the moment of creation are one. The classics exist not as sacred texts but as a rich mixture of forms, feelings, and vocabulary that each artist has thoroughly digested and made his or her own.

Like jazz, classical Indian music is created from traditional patterns and components: ragas and talas — scales, progressions, rhythms, improvisationally combined and merging together in the moment. Ravi Shankar, Ali Akbar Khan, and Nikhil Banerjee, pioneers who popularized Indian music in the West, were carrying on traditions taught by Khan's father, Allauddin Khan (1862–1972), stretching back before him to his ancestor Tansen (1506–1589), and then deep into the past of Vedic rhythms and intonations. Indian music is most appreciated by its fans when the performer is, in the same moment, faithfully transmitting an ancient practice and speaking with a fresh voice in the present. The ingredients are so deeply internalized through practice that they re-form into new constellations naturally, with little or no conscious thought.

• • •

Adams then rapped out a hundred Greek verses.
— Henry Fielding, *Joseph Andrews*

The rhythmic scaffoldings on which improvisers spin long-form creations appear in manifold varieties: the French alexandrine, the English iambic pentameter, the twelve-bar blues, the tightly crenulated rhymes of rap. Indian epics, like the *Mahabharata* and the *Ramayana*, were spun out in pairs of sixteen beat lines called *shlokas*. With electronic assistance, we play with loopers and digital or analog delays, using the pulse of the past second, the past five seconds, the past twenty-three seconds, five minutes ago, cycles of clock time as a skeleton to clamber and play over.

Pulse drives prose as well as poetry. For example, anaphora builds up rhythmic breaths by repeating an initial word or phrase. It dwells at the heart of compelling oration and storytelling. Anaphora, from the Greek αυφορά, or "carrying back" — go back, go back, repeat again, restart like a rondo, or the chorus of a rock song. We do it in music all the time: an initial riff is repeated, going each time in a different direction but each time returning, saying, Listen, here we are again. It is one of our ways of making waves in the mind. Martin Luther King made hypnotic poetry with the rhythm of his voice, in the deep tradition of African American preaching. Cued by Mahalia, he shifted seamlessly in midsentence from his written text making logical points to spontaneous speech. Music rose from those repetitions, taking us to a place that only art can: "I have a dream... I have a dream..." "Let freedom ring... Let freedom ring..."

Breath, heartbeat, footstep. Auditory, visual, tactile. All experience is marked by beats, rhythms, scaffolding, latticework. The fence around the redwood deck places musical bar lines on the sunlight, eight thin pickets, then a fat post. Twelve posts, ninety-six pickets wrapping around me, making a twelve- or ninety-six-step ladder. Here inside my body is the sequence of twenty-four vertebrae and twelve pairs of ribs that I play like an accordion with my breath, twenty thousand times a day, my seven neck bones, the seven neck bones of a giraffe, the twenty-six neck bones of a swan. Repetition, and repetition of the spaces between things, forms a rhythm of objects, visible everywhere in nature and invention. Rhythm is cross-sensory and everywhere around us.

Pulse may have longer wavelengths than we can perceive: beyond the rhythm of lines and beats, the wave of the total story, the wave of the day and year, the wave of one's total lifetime, waves that may not even seem like patterns until we see them from a certain vantage point.

• • •

Naamunaamuna is the person who accompanies a griot singer in West Africa among the Mandé-speaking peoples. His job is to shout *naamu!* (derived from the Arabic word meaning "yes") after each rhythmic line or natural breathing space in the recitation. The *naamu!* is soon taken up by the whole audience. The improvisation of the story is not just a performance "by" the virtuoso griot, with his or her fabulous ability to rap out rhythmic verse; it is a collective enterprise of the performer and the audience breathing as one, the shouts of the *naamunaamuna* egging the story on. Many languages and traditions have a version of this role. Audience-performer-audience-performer: the ritual interaction volleys back and forth. That is the real rhythm here, not just "inside" the tale but people speaking to each other. Think of the call-and-response in African American churches in which rhythmic preaching and shouts of "Amen! Say it!" cascade into a collective utterance.

The *naamunaamuna* — the "encouragers" — shout out words of cheer to keep the mastersinger in the flow. Yes, yes. Right on. It is a loop of mutual attention. Singer, encourager, and audience: all create the work together. This is why solo improvisers often feel that they can only play something interesting when people are present.

Lord described how the singers of traditionally impro-vised tales learn to let the narrative develop through a con-tinuous process of self-adjustment. Apprentice singers learn to use meter, to shift lines and story elements into place on the fly. Adjustment is recursive feedback — the fundamental process of learning and evolution. When we're not respon-sive to our environment, not interacting, the current stops and the life drains out.

• • •

Telling or inventing the bedtime story, our body comes equipped with enormous resources on which we can draw. We create our conversations, our music, our gestures and dances, with bodies that grew around a latticework of very old DNA. An alphabet of just four letters, the four com-ponent bases of DNA, generates combinations and per-mutations of immense variety. How unoriginal, to make everything out of formulaic building blocks — but it seems to have worked for three billion years. As organisms and as storytellers, we integrate elements old and new, borrowed and transposed, into something that evolves before our eyes. Improv, even of the traditional kind, is still creating new nev-er-to-be-repeated patterns, playing out through context and circumstance. Of the uncountable leaves in view on a moun-tainside, each one is of a type, yet each one is different. This is how nature and evolution improvise *us*.

• • •

I heard a classical scholar giving a paper about Odysseus the Improviser — one of Homer's epithets for him. Odysseus dealt with changes and setbacks as they arose, made up elab-orate lies and endless fake backstories filled with rich detail, rode away from a shipwreck on a log, constructed a home-made raft from materials that were there near the beach. As you can imagine, this was a subject of great interest to me. But the lecturer stood at a podium and read out loud his paper on improvisation, droning on and on, grinding a lively subject into something that tasted like sawdust. He clearly knew his business and could have simply told us about it. Perhaps he was afraid he might forget one of the points he intended to make. But if he knew twenty-five things and con-versationally told us only twenty of them, we never would have missed the other five. If he had started down one path and ended up on another, we would not have minded. If he had exhibited his human imperfection, that would have been all right too. After he finished reading his paper he sat down, and a woman stood to give the next talk. Rather than listen-ing to her, he sat there editing his script, repurposing it for an article while the event was still happening.

We give life to the script or kill it by our awareness of context and the breath and bodies of the people present. By *script* I am not referring to the presence or absence of writ-ing, but to the presence or absence of the person. Lincoln wrote the Gettysburg Address before delivering it. But he wrote it for that unique occasion, for the people gathered at Gettysburg in 1863, and that is why it survived as a work of power and beauty. He was so clear about what he needed to convey in that moment because he was present as a person to the enormity of the war, the stakes, the loss people were experiencing.

Speaking in the moment means seeing what the moment requires, whether the speech is prepared or improvised, whether the children's story is read from a book or invented on the spot. Yet as soon as we attempt to fix that speaking in a single form, we encounter the limits of notation. Even the Gettysburg Address, a short speech by one of the most well-documented people in history, exists in half a dozen different manuscript copies by Lincoln and his two secretaries, all of them slightly different. No one knows which is the "real" or definitive version.

• • •

The linguist Deborah Tannen suggested that instead of speaking of literacy versus orality, we speak of experience that emphasizes *content* versus experience that emphasizes *interaction*. And *interaction* does not necessarily mean that you are in the room with the other person. A novel by a dead author might grab us and propel us into an active and transformational dialogue. A speech we are listening to in the present moment can bore us and seem like an artifact from the land of the dead.

Teaching and learning are of their essence interactive and unpredictable experiences. The word *interactive* has been appropriated and diminished by the computer industry to mean selecting which predefined menu item to click. Industrial powers want us to click on *like* or *dislike* and be satisfied with that.

In the commerce of media, information can be quantified, bought and sold, converted into intellectual property, usurped, stolen, squeezed into online education. But learning is not an absorption of pure data, it's not a download to be completed; it's a living process that loses its essential dimension when reduced to a one-way relationship. Electronic media provide exquisite modalities of multisensory communication, but we need to use them in ways that enhance systemic and organic education instead of replacing it. Interactive learning means speaking together, playing to-gether, experimenting, conversing with friends, or moving and breathing in slow dialogue with a book, with the person-ality of the dead author, dwelling in the complexity of inter-mingling cultures. We can do that whether we are in the same room or on opposite sides of the globe. Rhythms of silence and memory wake up our mutual connections. Education should always be interactive, interpersonal, and exploratory. Where it will lead, no one can predict. Merely transmitting information is not teaching.

The art of teaching is a form of oral epic: telling a story, the same old story, a long story that unfolds over weeks, so that it is fresh and connected to what is happening here. If you are a good calculus teacher you will work with your evolving perceptions of who the students are and how the attention in the room develops, strengthens, and recedes. You will still use the textbook — but you tailor its lessons to the individuals present in the classroom. The needs of the students and their knowledge are going to be particular to them and to that place and time. You are putting together a fresh sequence for the people in this room, but this once-in-a-lifetime journey of this particular teacher and these partic-ular students will contain the narrative and the language of calculus.

In high school I had the privilege of taking classes from a man named J. E. Sparks. His course was simply called "Sem-inar." It took place in the morning before school started, in a conference room with about twenty kids sitting around the big table. We studied a wide range of philosophers like Plato and Spinoza, but also contemporary (1964) African politics. We read and wrote at home. But at the beginning of each class, Mr. Sparks looked around the room with his owlish eyes and softly said, "Books, books, books…" That meant, put your books and notebooks away; we will spend the next hour sitting across an empty table, looking at each other and discussing ideas. Sparks taught us to think together, to teach each other, without props. Long before mindfulness had migrated from Buddhism into popular practice, he was teaching it to us. A shared experience in a particular time and space. We were all in it together.

•   •   •

In the thirteenth century, St. Thomas Aquinas (of all people) asked "Whether Christ Should Have Committed His Doctrine to Writing." His answer was no — he suggested that Jesus preferred the intimacy and immediacy of oral teaching, offered to people in a particular place and time. Aquinas continued: "And so it was that among the gentiles, Pythagoras and Socrates, who were teachers of great excellence, were unwilling to write anything. For writings are ordained, as to an end, unto the imprinting of doctrine in the hearts of the hearers." By *doctrine* he seems to have meant what we would call dogma, fixing ideas into a misplaced concreteness — or misplaced abstraction. Paradoxically, St. Thomas was himself *writing*, in what would go on to be one of the most widely circulated and studied texts of all time, about the value of the unwritten and the unwritable. He goes on to say that if Christ's teachings were committed to writing, then there would not be space enough for them, since there were so many variants suited to different minds.

The Buddha, another historical figure who might have been on Aquinas's list had Aquinas known about him, is said to have given eighty-four thousand teachings, each pitched to the ears and understanding of his students, and to their particular setting. The versions that were written down by others and transmitted through multiple lineages fill volumes, but they are said to be but a helpful glimpse of the live experience. In the Buddhist tradition, such teaching is called *upaya* — skillful means. Enlightening mentors "knew the faculties of sentient beings," says the fourth-century Avatamsaka Sutra, "and taught them according to potential and necessity." A plethora of documents, some preserved, some lost, a multitude of viewpoints. Each of the early sutras begins with "Thus I have heard..." This gap between the recording of the teachings and the teachings themselves is not seen as a deficit among Buddhist monks and scholars but as a foregrounded element of the essential inability of the dharma to be fully delineated.

The text is not the teaching, but is often treated as such. It is easier to follow the letter than the spirit. No document or recording can capture the total reality from which it arose. From Aquinas's perspective, Jesus, Socrates, and Pythagoras chose to forgo the technology of written transmission because the oral transmission is too intimate and rich to be pinned down in a single representation. These significant teachers were not speaking once and for all to the ages, not speaking a fixed truth set in stone. They were speaking to you.

There is a fluid interaction between texts and oral transmission, and that interaction is the hallmark of a great deal of human culture. Western classical music depends heavily on notation. But the conductor Larry Livingston told me, "All notation has to be passed through the enlightening prism of your mind and the traditions of how it's done, which largely come from example and down from your teacher's teacher.

The one thing a score can never tell you about a piece is *how it goes*."

The dharma, whether it is Aquinas's scholastic Catholicism or Dōgen's Soto Zen, concentrates the mind on a reality that can only imperfectly be expressed in any one setting. Every expression is tied to person, place, and time. Context is everything. The important thing isn't to tell the perfect story. It is to tell the story the people in front of you need to hear. To do that, you must first understand who stands before you. In teaching, seeing and listening are at least as important as speaking. We must combine old and new, prefabricated and invented, transmission and absorption, blending seemingly opposite functions in the intimacy of mutual presence. That balancing act is the art of is.

·

· II ·

THINKING AS NATURE THINKS

Natural History

When you try to pick out anything by itself, you find it hitched to everything else in the universe.
— John Muir

Nouns: person, place, thing, idea. We treat all four as though they were solid objects with definite dimensions. But they are not. My violin is made of maple and spruce, with trimmings of ebony and boxwood. The forests in which those trees grew evolved over eons, through shifting ecological conditions. The rain, the insect vectors of plant life, the soil that is the substance of dead organisms (each with his or her own story), all played roles in the interactivity of coevolution. The vibrational characteristics of this wood are related to how it was cut, how it was cured before it was sold to an instrument maker, who in turn drew upon generations of training, art, and science in her craftsmanship. The instrument is a solid object but is also story upon story upon story. The varnish is its own story, made from minerals, resins, and organic compounds with their own past, present, and future. And eventually, in the fullness of time, the instrument will turn into debris and disappear. A dynamic, interactive system, not a thing.

In Buddhism this view is called the *emptiness of inherent existence*. When Westerners hear the word *emptiness*, we feel alarmed, because we think that emptiness means nihilism. The operative word in that phrase is *inherent*. The instrument is real and full of intricate happenings — biological, geological, cultural — full of labor, tradition, inventiveness, all interactive stories of great complexity. The one thing it is empty of is a separate, self-contained, self-sufficient existence.

I am holding a red guitar cable. Like the violin, the cable was made by people; the copper and steel, plastic and rubber came from many places and many stories; likewise the whole history of consciousness of the engineers who designed the cable, and the workers who labored on an assembly line factory in China. Each of those people has a past, present, and future, a family and friends and other relationships. They are employed by a company that has its own past, present, and future and is part of an environment of business and labor relations. Just those labor relations could give rise to a near infinity of stories, songs, and theater, protest and creative social action. We are looking at an immense nexus of interrelated activity, which is only temporarily present in the form of the "object" in my hand. Yet the object is eminently real — if I am playing onstage, I can step over the cable in the wrong way and trip. Emptiness is not the same as nonexistence.

Thich Nhat Hanh substitutes for *emptiness* a new word that is more precisely communicative in the West: *interbeing*. The wood of the instrument, the trees, the people who cultivated the trees, the people who crafted the instrument, the people who work in the factories who made the strings, the cable, and everything else, all of those inter-are with the violin or the cable.

There is a wonderful third-century text from China called Hsi K'ang's *Poetical Essay on the Lute*. It is about playing an instrument called the *guqin*. While Hsi K'ang does talk about musical things like scales and technique and timing, he devotes a large part of his text to describing the mountains and forests where the catalpa trees grow, the streams and mists that nourish them. "The trees which lutes are built to grow on the lofty ridges of steep mountains. For a thousand years they wait for him who shall recognize their value, quietly they repose, forever robust." For Hsi K'ang, the proper study of a musician is ecology — the ecology of the forest, and also the social ecology, the intellectual ecology from which the instrument arises. This observation extends even further. On finishing the instrument, we tune it up — and tuning is yet another world of interactivity and history, where our physical sensations engage with a mixture of mathematical and cultural forms. Then we finally begin to strum it, engrossing ourselves in the ecology of our everyday sensorium — the interactive physiology of muscles, bones, nerves, the ways in which body movement creates sound and the way sound is reflected in the room and in nature. This landscape includes tunes rattling around in our heads, from the commercial we heard on the radio this morning to some piece of music we have always loved. All these things coexist with the present moment of our real-time artistic creation, and they are available for us to draw on.

The practice of improvising allows us to *play with* impermanence and interbeing. Person, place, thing, and idea are contingent on context. If you are sitting in a chair, you have a lap. Now stand up, and you don't have a lap.

Emptiness of *inherent* existence: the guitar cable or the improvisation doesn't exist by itself, but it coexists, it inter-is, with the air, the ear, the physics of vibration, histories, and social relations. And because of that interbeing, we can stand up with nothing up our sleeves, no plans and no stated intentions, and improvise music with each other. Such experience is possible because an infinite amount of information to draw on is already present and already with us, from the three billion years of organic evolution immanent in our bodies to the evolution of our cultures, our friends' cultures, all the patterns with which we have come into contact.

We could spend years exploring the chemistry, physics, sociology, economics, biology, industrial design, and all the interconnected fields of existence implicated in the making and playing of the violin and cable. We could run an entire university from the study of either.

This is no vague statement that "everything is one" — it is an invitation to see at least some of the myriad, minutely delineated interconnections present in everything we look at. Each interconnection is a story. As we look at the ecology of the forest or the city, we see that each is made of infinitely accumulating stories. Thus the old-fashioned term for biology: *natural history*.

I see improvising as a tool for investigating reality. What is this reality that we are investigating? It is the reality of interbeing, the opposite of thingness. This mutuality is the engine that powers our natural improvisational activity. I once asked Gregory Bateson, "What is beauty?" He answered, "Recognition of the pattern which connects."

People are more dynamic and ever-changing than guitar cables or violins, yet we have been trained to cherish the idea of the independent, isolated individual. Then we experience a catastrophe — pollution, climate change, terrorism, war — and suddenly we discover that human beings need each other. The idea of the independent, isolated individual is encapsulated in the nineteenth-century image of the composer, artist, or author sitting alone and creating works of genius from nothing. This image feeds right into the idea of music history as masterpieces hanging from the clothesline of time — an image that is obsolete and has never fit the realities of natural history.

·

All About Frogs

One afternoon I was giving a talk at a university religion department. My host asked me to talk about the Tao, creativity, and music. I wanted to begin with a little meditation. In this crowded classroom full of random furniture and people, we managed to get silent and still, allowed ourselves to become comfortable wherever we were — sitting in chairs, squatting on the floor, standing straight, sitting on someone's lap, leaning on a ledge. Settled and quiet, we found our balance and let the concerns and preoccupations that we had brought with us leak away. I felt like a pendulum freed from outside impulse, swinging more and more slowly, less and less erratically, gradually coming to rest.

Imperceptibly, we became conscious of a bass hum in the heating system as it whirred away in the ceiling. In the silence of this room, the sound of the motor became very strong. Normally, while talking and listening, thinking and worrying, we don't notice such noises. That motor reminded me of a wonderful realization I'd had in the hotel room where I'd slept the previous night. There was a rickety little refrigerator in the room and, as refrigerators do, it turned on and off as its thermostat switched in and out. I was lying in bed, feeling tense, almost unaware of the low, rattling drone, when suddenly *pop!* — the refrigerator turned off. The machine's noise was subtle, but its cessation was like the moment in old slapstick movies when someone has been beating you over the head and then stops. How good it feels! The acute silence that occurred when the refrigerator shut off was beautiful, as I lay there in the dark smiling with contentment. It sounds silly. But spiritual realization is often sparked by the most humdrum events.

As we sat in our afternoon meditation, someone coughed. What was amazing, and just as silly as the refrigerator, was how beautiful and resonant that cough sounded. When we're going about our business and someone coughs, it's just noise, a distraction; but against the background of silent concentration we shared, that cough was a marvelous sound that expanded into the universe. It lasted only half a second, but we could hear the different phases of the cough so that it became something rather intricate and interesting. Later on, we will return to the cough and the silence of the refrigerator because they are of fundamental significance to our purpose.

• • •

Now let's talk about frogs. In the late 1950s at MIT, Humberto Maturana, Jerome Lettvin, and others were trying to figure out how vision works at the level of single nerve and brain cells, how *information* arises from the raw stimulus of light and darkness. In particular they were studying the retina and visual cortex of frogs. They invented tiny, hair-like electrodes that could detect the firing of a single nerve cell. With such electrodes in place, they showed various visual stimuli to the animals, to see which cells fire under what conditions.

One of the seminal papers that came out of this research was called "What the Frog's Eye Tells the Frog's Brain." Previously we had thought of the eye as though it were a camera that passively takes in patterns of light; the information about the light is transferred up into the brain, which then does processing on it and distinguishes faces, letters of the alphabet, all the things we are used to recognizing. In the case of the frog, the recognition happens before the signals even get to the brain, in the nerve cells of the retina at the back of the eye. These cells are predisposed to fire most strongly when they detect small, dark dots moving around. This, of course, is because frogs eat flies. Finding flies is vitally important to frogs, and what the frog's eye tells the frog's brain is whether or not flies seem to be present. Everything else is secondary. The researchers put various types of stimuli in front of the frogs — big, open areas of color or different shapes with different rates of movement — and they would all produce some mild excitation in the nerve cells in the eye. But the nerve cells would really start jumping around when something was presented that could have been a fly: a moving black dot that subtends about one degree of angle.

Before the information even gets to the brain, the frog's eye has an epistemology. *Epistemology* normally refers to the theory of knowledge: a branch of philosophy that asks,

How do we know? What do we know? What is real? What is important? How do we sort our inputs into knowledge versus nonsense? Gregory Bateson transplanted this word into biology, realizing that even a rat in a learning experiment has an epistemology, an internalized theory of knowledge that calibrates its perceptual biases. Epistemology thus becomes greatly extended in meaning, to an activity inherent in all sentient beings. Neural filtering sensitizes a frog's eye to movements of small dots that are likely to be flies and disregards other information. Epistemology is how we parse the world: *this* is information, *that* is noise. Likewise, cultural filtering predisposes a person to believe or disbelieve in miracles, or in economic determinism. In an age pervaded by propaganda, epistemology has suddenly turned into an explicit preoccupation of our entire society: what we know, what is real, what is important.

Imagine a pond at sunset, the beautiful lily pads, the blazing sky, the frog. The frog sits there thinking, "Not-flies."

We humans believe ourselves to be much grander than frogs. We are general-purpose organisms who can adapt to many settings. We don't have a frog's specific hardwiring for flies, but nevertheless human retinas are hardwired to spot edges and differences. When we look around a room, our retinal ganglion cells fire more strongly when they see borders and contours than when they see the blank middle areas of uniform color. As the information gets bumped up through higher levels of brain cells, those edges yield more information — tuned by our predispositions. We are sensitive to the outlines, because that's where the news is. A blank piece of paper may not contain much to attract us, but if we draw a single line across it, now *there's* a piece of information and our eye gravitates there. The line has divided the field into two pieces. Information is measured in bits or binary digits, a single distinction. So this mark creates one bit of information — either yes or no, on or off, one or zero, this side of the line or that side. In the light of common themes from logic, philosophy, neurology, psychology, and computer design, Bateson established that the fundamental unit or atom of mind is a single *difference*.

In the Bible, the universe begins with a single binary distinction. "Let there be light" cleaves the unformed void into light and darkness, and everything develops from there. If you look at the first page of Genesis — the page that is consonant with the theory of evolution — we see more advanced life-forms evolving from less advanced forms. By *advanced* I mean more differentiated. First there's the division between light and darkness. Then the division between above and below. Then the division between wet and dry; between land and sea; living things and nonliving things; plants and animals; and you know how it goes, by powers of two. After three or four billion years of divisions, you are a complex, sentient organism, composing a book about your life's work. It all stems from one distinction, one binary division, one mark on a blank page.

• • •

Now leap from the realm of retinas, brain cells, and epistemology to a frog painting by Sengai, the great Japanese painter-priest (1750–1837). Frogs were a favorite subject of Zen and Taoist masters throughout the centuries. This painting is partly a comment on the famous haiku by Bashō (1643–1694):

old pond —
frog jumps in.
Plop!

That *Plop!* is like the
moment of shocking, blissful clarity that came for me
in the middle of the night
when the steady background
noise of the refrigerator suddenly ceased. Or, yet again, from
Genesis, "Let there be light" — that stark moment of illumi-
nation, literal enlightenment, when something arises from
nothing and the universe comes into being. *Plop!* is Bashō's
Zen equivalent of "Let there be light," a moment of creativity that is potentially available to us anytime, right before our
eyes, right under our fingertips. But usually we are too busy
looking out for flies, or lamenting their absence.

In the case of "what the frog's eye tells the frog's brain,"
there is a predisposition to see the universe in terms of one
question. That question is hardwired right into the nerve
cells of the frog's eyes, and for good survival reasons, for
frogs must eat. But there is much this limited epistemology
excludes: the clarity of cool water refracting light, the generations and empires of pond scum sliding over rocks, hungry
birds circling above for frog-shaped dinner.

Many institutions have their own version of the frog's
eyes, parsing the universe in terms of a single question, "Is
there a profit there? What's the bottom line?" while ignoring
the proverbial birds. This is how we end up fouling our own
environment in pursuit of short-term return on investment.

Thus we see weapons industry lobbyists with senators in their pockets. This is how people can get so focused on accumulating money that they don't realize it isn't making them any happier. There is nothing wrong with pursuing profit. However, pursuing it at the expense of all else harms the social fabric and is deeply self-destructive. If we operate within an unexamined epistemology, then our choices are made for us in advance — like the frog's brain vibrating with excitement on seeing a fly. We may not even realize how constricted our perceptions (and thus our actions) are without investigating their basis and the assumptions they contain.

Life depends on our transcending the premises that have confined us. The crucial moment is identifying them. Freedom from our presuppositions is and always has been an option. That realization is the *Plop!* of Bashō's frog.

We don't need to take exotic journeys to realize this experience. It is available to us here, now, at every instant of our lives. In meditation, in the practices of art and science and other pursuits when undertaken creatively, we attempt to get behind and before the epistemological distinctions that we normally accept. We are trying to get back to what was on that piece of paper before we drew our line. What face did you have before you were born — before all those millions and trillions of cell divisions?

Here is a text by Seng-Ts'an, the Third Patriarch of Zen in China, called the "Hsin Hsin Ming" ("Verses on the Truthful Mind"):

> *The Great Way is not difficult*
> *just avoid picking and choosing.*
> *When love and hate are both absent*

everything becomes clear and undisguised.
Make the smallest distinction, however,
and heaven and earth are set infinitely apart.
If you wish to see the truth
then hold no opinions for or against anything.
To set up what you like against what you dislike
is the disease of the mind.
When the deep meanings of things are not understood
the mind's essential peace is disturbed to no avail.

The Way is perfect like vast space
where nothing is lacking and nothing is in excess.
Indeed, it is due to our choosing to accept or reject
that we do not see the true nature of things.

We are looking at strange and wonderful puzzles here. Seng-Ts'an is saying that you can find the Great Way not by going beyond preferences but by having no preferences. This, of course, is a paradox: you actively chose to open to this page at this moment, and that's why we are here listening to Seng-Ts'an talk about how eye-opening it is to have no preferences. We had preferences to put on certain clothes this morning, to take every step that led us to this moment. Life is compounded of preferences. Every time we open our mouths we express preferences. Hardwired as our brain cells seem to be, we can get beneath that programming to a place of seeing freshly, as though for the first time — and noticing that we often make choices without even realizing.

We all have had the contrary experience, of having our understanding of something *stopped* by knowing the name for it. When Ronald Reagan was running for governor of

California in 1966, he stated, "If you've seen one redwood tree, you've seen them all." This was his justification for allowing the logging companies to come in and chop down forests of thousand-year-old sequoias. From his limited point of view, he was right, because as soon as you put the label *tree* on a natural phenomenon, you begin to see the name and not the thing itself. It is easy to look around the world, put names and concepts on things, and dismissively say, "I know what that is, I've heard that before, it's old hat." In 1799 Blake wrote, "The tree which moves some people to tears of joy is in the eyes of others only a green thing that stands in the way."

Today we know that a tree in a forest is not a single entity at all but a member of a widely interdependent and interactive community of many species. Everyone knows that a tree is a tree, but it is quite another thing to actually walk into the redwood forest and see the unique, minutely delineated structure of each of those ancient living beings, to see them as individual elements in the amazing ecological system in which you are standing, to see how the tiny insects and the huge sequoias are feeding each other, to see how all the species of plants and animals are interconnected into a single biological circuit so intricate that if you take one piece out, the whole system can collapse. If you place a simple ticket of identity on the redwood tree, then the tree loses the richly detailed fabric of its being and its context. The consequences are immense, because in your mental stuckness you give permission for the forest to be killed, and the costs of that act of killing flow back disastrously to affect the viability of entire species, including ours.

• • •

Back to frogs. The world becomes dangerously simple if all you're looking for, all your epistemology encompasses, is flies or not-flies. The frog can be tricked into swallowing other moving dark objects that are not flies. Human beings are just as easily deceived. We greedily swallow many things

that are not nourishment. One antidote to an unbalanced epistemology is practice, in its many forms. We can practice going behind our predispositions to experience the nature of our own minds. We can practice by walking in a forest or by a tide pool, learning the intricacy that is in front of us, without a priori placing labels on it. At some point we may want to communicate our experience to other people — and to do that, we use words, labels, and concepts. We can enjoy the delicious, variegated play of concepts given to us by our languages and all our academic traditions — but we can learn to use them in a provisional way, understanding that we are looking at a map of reality and not at reality itself.

"There is nothing either good or bad," says Shakespeare's Hamlet, "but thinking makes it so."

The Maturana-Lettvin experiments reveal the normal functioning not just of frogs or isolated neural preparations but of ourselves. Like the frog, we are looking not at reality but at a map of reality that predisposes us to see in a certain way. Bashō's *Plop!* is about breaking through perceptual and experiential barriers. *Plop!* is the sound of breaking through the surface of things so we can see and hear more. The surface of the pond is the surface of consciousness — the mysterious watery barrier between reflection and reality.

Psychologists in the time of William James coined the term *anoetic sentience* to describe this state of mind — in other words, sentience that is without  or is prior to cognitive processing. It can be an eye-opening revelation to simply *be* where we are, to see and hear what's here without putting labels on it. We can experience the difficulty of this if we look around us as we go through our day. We cannot help recognizing the faces of our friends; we know that a chair is a chair, and we know many things through the elaborate concepts and shortcuts that have been trained into us. Yet it is possible to some extent, provisionally and for a while, to go underneath that level of experience. Anoetic sentience is literally impossible, but we can get a bit closer to it than we usually are, eliminate some barriers, some surfaces, see a little more cleanly and deeply, become a little less muddled by the mind's constant activity of picking and choosing.

Anoetic sentience is a paradox, because if we were to somehow neutralize all our neural, educational, cultural, and evolutionary wiring and see just what's "out there" — the thing-in-itself, as Kant called it, we would discover that thing-out-there to be empty of inherent existence. This is the fundamental insight of Buddhism, *shunyata*, the emptiness of inherent existence. The existence of things is not *inherent* in each but rather *interdependent*. Everything exists in a network of interdependence with every other element of the universe through complex chains of cause and effect (karma). Perhaps the best model we now have for understanding this is the notion of ecosystem. The existence of the pond depends on everything else, including the rigid wiring of the frog's retinal ganglion cells. That is why Ronald Reagan's notion of redwood trees is the most destructive and at the same time most common epistemological error. The English physicist David Bohm tells us: "Of course, there is a real need for thought and language momentarily to focus attention on one thing or another, as the occasion demands. But when each such thing is regarded as separately existent and essentially independent of the broader context of the whole in which it has its origin, its sustenance, and its ultimate dissolution, then one is no longer merely focusing attention, but, rather, one is engaged in breaking the field of awareness into disjoint parts, whose deep unity can no longer be perceived."

• • •

I have found that music is a profound path to going behind that kind of processing, because it is essentially and fundamentally nonverbal, empty of the utilitarian meanings and purposes for which our frog's eye is always scanning.

Many people play instruments, sometimes beautifully and with great skill, under the illusion that they are playing "notes." Here are two completely different words made of the same four letters: *n-o-t-e* and *t-o-n-e*. A *tone* is the actual sound that you make on an instrument, the actual sound that we hear — the sound of the refrigerator or the cough we talked about earlier. A *note* is a notation. It's a little symbol that we might call "B-flat." It is specific to Western culture, does not necessarily have any meaning in another culture, and doesn't have any meaning in terms of sound waves; it is a way of classifying a tone and communicating it to other people. If you play an instrument like the violin, or the double bass, or the slide trombone, or your vocal cords, which are analog instruments that can be varied continuously, you discover that "B-flat" actually represents an infinite range of tones. It's easy to see this on a big instrument like the double bass because the strings are so long. You put your finger down on the string here for a B-flat and there for a B. The distance between B-flat and B is a couple of inches. What's going on in those inches? Is it no-man's-land? No. There is a continuous variation of finger positions and tones; they're all real sounds whether or not they have names in our particular symbol system. The cracks between two adjacent piano keys hide fine gradations of tone, which a tempered instrument like the piano cannot play. The symbol system cannot contain the musical reality.

When a frog jumps into a pond, the surface radiates waves and ripples. The plop makes neither a B nor a B-flat, though we the observers may classify the sound that way after the fact; we transform sound into Bs and B-flats just as the frog's eye and nervous system transform patterns of light into flies and not-flies.

Music to some extent is described by a symbol system, but the real music, the actual sound that we hear, cannot be described. It can only be experienced. A riff on the piano or saxophone is utterly meaningless, hence utterly real. *Plop!* Down we drop, to that deep pool of anoetic sentience, before news of the fly enters the frog's eye and brain, before the first distinction separating the first light from the first darkness — our act of creative engagement dips us into that realm of unclassified direct experience. Attempts to talk about this are necessarily clumsy and inadequate. This direct experience is attainable to some extent through music and other artistic modalities. It is attainable through dreams and myth, which undercut the limitations of consciousness and go to a deeper level. You may ask if it is ever possible to listen to music without some type of thinking or classification. On hearing a piece of music we instantly think of categories: classical or country, Indian raga or Japanese gagaku. A highly trained musician may have trouble listening to any piece of music without analyzing the rhythms and harmonies. But while music rests partly in a cognitive and cultural space, it is also pure sound, indescribable and indefinable. An arm of the music dips us into the anoetic or spiritual space of *emptiness*. That's where the known is commingled with the unknown.

· · ·

We are constantly being taught by small children about how continually surprising, malleable, and funny our universe is, how easily we can see things from a new angle. Here is a verse from the great Taoist Chuang Tzu that I would like to add to the images we've been contemplating. He has Lao Tzu say to an apprentice:

> *Can you become a little child?*
> *The child will cry all day, without its throat becoming*
> *   hoarse; — so perfect is the harmony of its physical*
> *   constitution.*
> *It will keep its fingers closed all the day without relaxing their*
> *   grasp; — such is the concentration of its powers.*

It will keep its eyes fixed all day, without their moving;
— so is it unaffected by what is external to it.
It walks it knows not where; it rests where it is placed, it
knows not why; it is calmly indifferent to things,
and follows their current.

Lao Tzu's disciple asks, "Is this perfection?" Babies are inspiring, they point us to a profound kind of bliss, but should we just laugh and cry, indiscriminately sticking anything and everything into our mouths, and forget everything we have learned through our schooling and our experience as grown-ups? In Zen art there are many pictures of frogs, partly because the sitting frog looks like a person sitting in zazen posture. The Sengai frog painting we examined earlier has a double meaning: yes, the frog jumps in and makes his *Plop!* but Sengai added an inscription to his painting stating that if all there was to spiritual attainment were sitting contentedly and naturally, then frogs would themselves be enlightened buddhas. My baby sons needed an adult to help them discriminate between swallowing food and swallowing thumbtacks. Is this perfection?

Lao Tzu replies, "No. This is what we call breaking the ice." It is only the beginning. We cannot avoid growing up and developing our minds, and it is unquestionably good to discriminate between nourishment and its opposite. Still, let us try to recover, to some extent, the vast consciousness of the infant, who sees everything for the first time. This baby-consciousness melts the ice on the path to real mastery, so that we are able, finally, to be grown-ups, know what we know, use language, use experience, but do so in an open, provisional, easygoing fashion that allows us to see what is really in front of us.

William Blake taught that we find enlightenment in the "minute particulars" of creation, like a child closely studying the worms and bugs and frogs, freshly seeing the details that are there, unclouded by our programming, our "mind-forged manacles." Keys to awareness are ever-present, in the simplest things. The  great ninth-century Zen master Chao-chou asked his teacher, "What is the Way?" Nan-chuan replied, "Your ordinary mind is the Way." That is why I have devoted so much time to talking about refrigerator noise and a cough.

The cough that I found so instructive when we did our little meditation at the beginning of these pages could, in another context, have been just an annoyance. But instead it was something exquisite, like the cessation of the refrigerator noise. *Plop!*

The composer John Cage was famous for his view that all the sounds around us can be music, and for inspiring many other artists to expand the possibilities of what and how they might create. Cage lived in New York City, and to him the engine sounds, the honking and the screaming and everything else, were music. He believed we live in a continuous texture of noise-as-music. One afternoon I was visiting John, and as an ambulance screamed past, he said to me, "When I was younger, I used to be interested in sounds like traffic noise and sirens. But now that I'm old I'm interested in more subtle sounds like the refrigerator turning on and off." As he said that, I inwardly scoffed, "Well, that's very nice, John, but I still get more pleasure listening to Sonny Rollins play 'Autumn Nocturne' than listening to the rumbling of the washing machine." At best I found his words a rather charming statement, made by a man who understood how to be at peace with the universe. But I was wrong; it was more than a charming statement. I never understood what John was saying until that night in the hotel room ten years later, when the refrigerator turned off and the silence was delicious.

Buddhists speak of the Third Noble Truth, the cessation of suffering. Suffering, great and small, is an inherent part of life, but it can lift, the moment we wake up through clarifying mind and seeing what is before us: a complex world of interdependent, coevolving beings that cannot be contained by names and concepts, cannot be pinned down as flies or not-flies, profit or not-profit. *Buddha* means "one who woke up." The cessation of the refrigerator noise was the tiny cessation of a tiny suffering. Yet through these little teachings of everyday life we wake up and know that such cessation is possible. *Pop!* goes the refrigerator, *plop!* goes the frog, and we wake up.

That cessation was a musical sound in itself, the sound of silence, with its own beauty, like the cough that resonated through our meditation earlier. When we quiet ourselves and tune up our senses, every sound, or the cessation thereof, is crisp and clear.

Bashō's frog may or may not have found flies, but with an exquisite startling little noise he *Plop*ped into that pond, breaking through the reflective surface of mind and nature. Bashō woke up, and we with him.

•

Twists and Turns

> *Unpremeditated music is the true gauge which*
> *measures the current of our thoughts, the very*
> *undertow of our life's stream.*
> — Henry David Thoreau

Sing O Muse of whatever comes to mind. Begin anywhere and follow the flow. There's no telling where you might be swept off to. The improvisational process is rooted in free association — and the near guarantee that after a while, free association will turn up significant patterns. Even the most trivial thoughts can lead to a network of connections. The first gesture, sound, word, brushstroke, or thought may seem arbitrary, but it reminds you of *this*; *this* suggests *that*; *that* suggests the next thing. The pieces start fitting together. After a period of wandering, you may find yourself standing in a strange place that turns out to be your ancestral home-land — to encounter your original nature and know it for the first time.

Freud developed this simple and childish game into a tool of great power and elegance. In the free play of words, thoughts, feelings, and images, we need not be looking for repressed memories, for answers to life's conundrums, or for great art; we can allow spontaneous answers to take us someplace meaningful. The "free" of free association does not mean wild or random but free of deliberate purpose. No association is free of context and meaning, but it may reveal deeper truth if it is free of conscious (and often fearful) control.

As a teenager Freud was influenced by the essays of Ludwig Börne (born Loeb Baruch, 1786–1837), especially an essay called "The Art of Becoming an Original Writer in Three Days." Börne suggests, "Take a stack of paper and write. Write everything that goes through your mind for three consecutive days with neither hesitation nor hypocrisy. Write down what you think of yourself, of the Turkish war, of Goethe, of a criminal case, of the Last Judgment, of your boss — and when the three days are over you will be amazed at what novel and startling thoughts have spilled out of you." This prescription for spontaneous prose (prefiguring Baudelaire, Breton, Ginsberg, ruth weiss, Dorothea Brande, and many others) is not automatic writing, which is supposedly dictation from spirits, but dictation from ourselves: our own spirit. Write, noodle on a musical instrument or toy, doodle on the piece of paper until it gives up its secrets. You can refine it later. The output may not be something you want to share publicly (the delete button and the trash can are always available), but once unblocked you can start your journey in earnest.

Börne wrote, "To do this there is nothing one needs to learn, only much one needs to unlearn." And, "A shameful and cowardly fear of thinking holds every one of us back."

• • •

Methought I was enamored of an ass.
> — Shakespeare,
> *A Midsummer Night's Dream*

Free association is also free ass: you are free to make an ass of yourself. If I'm afraid of this freedom, I won't get up in the morning because I am sure to make an ass of myself at least a few times a day. Onstage and performing improvised music, the risk is nothing compared with my fumbles and mistakes in everyday life. Improvising thrives on our imperfection and how we integrate it into the flow of our activity. Everyone has problems, everyone is a mystery to him- or herself, everyone at some point begins to explore mind and feelings and relationships in some way, attempting to see the patterns that got us where we are. "I come," Blake wrote, "to cleanse the Face of my Spirit by Self-examination." By giving ourselves a space in which to slough off the veneer of perfection or professionalism, we can reach our next evolutionary step.

Freedom to make an ass of yourself might mean that your improvisation goes nowhere. It might peter out or go around in circles. In the creative context, as in the therapeutic one, it might mean bringing up awkward or humiliating material. We may feel that we are wasting our time with the music that wanders, the writing that no one will ever see, the drawing that we crumple up and throw away — but without these episodes we would never produce anything of quality. Vulnerability is a precondition of creative work.

• • •

> Our age is seeking a new spring of life. I found one and drank of it and the water tasted good.
>
> — C. G. Jung

Journeys may start with free association, but they don't end that way. We discover a direction and follow it. We draw, write, paint, sing our way into clarity, into connections to other people, into the workings of nature. Themes of which we had long been unconscious gradually come into focus, like islands emerging in the distance.

Carl Jung, after his break with Freud, extended the practice of free association to include hands-on modes of artistic creation. He called his method *active imagination*, allowing ideas and correlations to take tangible shape through visualization. For Jung, the practice took the form of painting and writing; for other people, it takes the form of music, theater, crafts, tinkering with technologies and expressive arts of all sorts, old and new. Freud's free association is a mode of mental-verbal exploration. Jung's active imagination is a concrete mode of doing, making, creating. His was an enterprise of knowing the self in order to transcend it. It is a journey of revelation: uncovering patterns within and around us that cannot be seen or even known until we manifest them. "The patient can make himself creatively independent through this method. He is no longer dependent on his dreams or on his doctor's knowledge; instead, by painting himself he gives shape to himself."

In his own life Jung practiced this method of exploration in his massive work of fantasy, myth, painting, and calligraphy. The *Red Book*, created during World War I, is an illuminated manuscript that looks like it tunneled here straight from the Middle Ages. The *Red Book* was known about for decades but only published fifty years after Jung's death. While leading a busy life practicing psychiatry, training analysts from around the world, and writing books, Jung managed to devote years to the arts of building, stonemasonry, and carving. Over decades he built a stone house with four towers at Bollingen on the shore of Lake Zurich, like a structure out of ancient times, new wings added as he discovered new patterns in his own personality, externalizing them in stone, in the form of alchemical carvings and other psychic symbols. On his seventy-fifth birthday in 1950, Jung made his way down to the lake, and with his wrinkled hands chiseled into the rock a fragment from Heraclitus: "Time is a child at play, gambling; a child's is the kingship."

Craftsmanship elevating personal evolution to a universal scale is also reflected in the dreamlike Watts Towers in Los Angeles, *Nuestro Pueblo*, seventeen enormous spirals stretching skyward, covered with mosaics made mostly from what had been trash, hand-built by Simon Rodia from 1921 to 1954. This was not practical, it was not economical. But it was the expression and discovery of life, and without that, what is there, mere survival?

An image pulls us into an interconnected network of patterns. Suddenly a fresh universe of thought and feeling is born. Curiosity and wonder motivate us to persevere. These pathways become a portal into Indra's net: the jeweled lattice of interrelations that encompasses the cosmos but is reflected from myriad points of perception.

Free association is the booster rocket, allowing us to attain escape velocity. But with active imagination, we eventually find ourselves gravitating elsewhere, to a center that draws us in, and we start firing thrusters to navigate toward that place and explore it.

The work of active imagination allows us to bridge the gaps between conscious and unconscious, logic and fantasy. It opens pathways to collective patterns we share with other people. Follow impulse in creative expression, see where it leads, let images unfold into an extended drama. We go from island hopping to pursuing a story with a shape. We find our unique linkage to nature, culture, and psyche.

Improvising is *inductive*. Whether a monologue or a conversation with partners, it moves in time from tone to tone, word to word, form to form. Looking back at the improvisation, we feel the inevitability of the pattern as though it were intentional. In collective improvising or conversation, the inductive paths of two or more people thread around each other like strands of a double helix, open-ended and relational, mutually reinforcing and contrasting. Thus we follow the poetic process of research by which links are tracked, threads woven, as in Blake:

> I give you the end of a golden string,
> Only wind it into a ball:
> It will lead you in at Heaven's gate,
> Built in Jerusalem's wall.

Jung knew his paintings were not "art" in the normal sense but a vehicle for investigation. He discovered that as he relentlessly excavated into the most deeply personal material, he began to identify archetypes, universal patterns shared among many cultures. Paradoxically, the deeper we venture into the roots of the self, the closer we come to transcending our self-centeredness, precisely because what we discover is how inseparable we are from the total structure of being.

In ancient times people described certain experiences as visits from gods and goddesses. In *The Odyssey* the goddess Athena appears to young Telemachus disguised as an older man named Mentor, his father's friend, to guide and help him. The same goddess whispers words into the ear of his long-missing father, Odysseus, on his ten-year journey home. Athena is the voice of inspiration; without her mastery and cleverness at devising tactics, Odysseus would never have taken back his home. Thus we now speak of having a mentor, an adviser, one who has taken particular interest in our story, in guiding us through our unique journey.

· · ·

Odysseus's intention was simple: sail back to his family when the Trojan War was over. He had the goal, the ships, the men: it was supposed to take a couple of weeks. But it took ten extra years. If he had carried out his plan successfully, no one would be telling his story three thousand years later. Our purposes are one thing; our actual adventures are something else entirely.

· · ·

Take a walk, anywhere. One step at a time, finding out where you are going by going there. Be led by a dog into a forest. He drags you along hard, and you go where his nose goes. Get lost in the middle of the road of life (Dante) and make underground and supernal discoveries; be blown off course by an angry god (Odysseus), or simply wander down the ordinary streets of your middle-class city (Leopold Bloom), and unforeseeable connections will spring up and surround you.

Our explorations take on the character of a journey to strange parts, which becomes a journey home. "I give you the end of a golden string, only wind it into a ball..." Golden strings of association, threads of awareness, spin themselves into stories. Spin strands into yarns, yarn into multidimensional patterns, like Bach's *Chaconne*. This monumental work for solo violin is often experienced as a journey there and back again. A motif of four descending tones, three beats each, repeating over and over with sixty-four variations, that's all it is, but it takes us through myriad territories, wild, exuberant, terrifying, joyful, excavating under the earth, soaring, and finally, repeating the initial theme, with a depth that can only be understood through the journey itself, all to a steady, slow pulse. Penelope spends three years weaving and unweaving, weaving and unweaving a shroud for her father-in-law, spinning a lie to deceive the suitors, to string them along and save herself. Scheherazade jumps from story to story for a thousand and one nights to save herself, stitching the strands of one into the next. We pick up the tools of our chosen art and shape tones and syllables into an unfolding plot. The string is spun out in time as a linear sequence, but in retrospect it feels inevitable.

We mischaracterize the act of finding pattern in seemingly separate facts as "connecting the dots." That metaphor implies that facts are separate entities, dots that stay still on a page. But each event is a wriggling thread of interactivity in spacetime, with its own past, present, and future. We spin them, or watch them spin themselves, into patterns that cannot be predicted.

Improvising is not "just" fantasy and imagination; it is what happens when our intentions meet the real world, with all its unpredictability. We smack into the limitations of materials and our abilities to manipulate those materials, the limitations of our relationships with other people, our collaborators or our opponents. *Then* what do we do? How do we pick ourselves up, change our shape, learn to do new or old tricks?

Homer gave us Odysseus, "the master improviser," "man of twists and turns," wearing countless costumes and shapes as he seeks to merge back into the simple life he once had. Though he arrives at his destination and reclaims his home, we speak of an odyssey as the journey itself, not as reaching a goal. We still follow his wanderings over the swarming sea, making up lies and stories to save his skin and cover his tracks, yarns that are still retold with pleasure three millennia later. Improvisational actor, his wily wife and son actors too, imagination guided by a gray-eyed goddess wearing the body and bearing the voice of a man called Mentor.

·

Listening

*Take a walk at night. Walk so silently that
the bottoms of your feet become ears.*
— Pauline Oliveros

To improvise, listen. You need nothing else. A friend who runs a children's theater came to a concert of improvised music. She later said that she had never seen two adults paying attention to each other as intently as she had that evening. When the music has no score, then listening is the score.

We listen not only with ears but through the full sensorium: eyes, nose, tongue, skin, body, mind. Muscles listen. Dianna Linden, one of the gurus of massage therapy, often spoke of *palpatory intelligence* — touching consciously, feeling the system of a particular body and adjusting accordingly. Evelyn Glennie, the world's foremost classical percussion soloist, is deaf. She hears through the soles of her feet, her whole body. It is a remarkable experience to watch her give a master class in contemporary percussion. While following a score, she is intently perceiving the student's sound, able to clue him or her in to hidden subtleties of expression.

Playing a violin or building one, playing with or building anything, we flow with a universe of feedback: kinesthetics, pressure sensitivity in the fingertips, temperature, the cochlear organ's ever-shifting sense of balance, and sense modalities that have no name.

• • •

In a study published in the *Annals of Internal Medicine* in 1984, investigators timed how long doctors listened to a patient before interrupting. The average was eighteen seconds.

I often think back to a conversation with a dear friend, Michael Stulbarg, a pulmonologist at UC San Francisco, who died in 2004. In the mid-1980s I asked him, "What do improvisation and creativity mean to you, in medicine?" Michael was what we used to call a left-brained person: scientific, rational, and logical. But he responded without hesitation. He said that improvisation is seeing and dealing with the actual patient in front of you rather than "treating the chart." Michael's response gives new meaning to the job title *attending physician*. I've talked to doctors many times since then and have often gotten some variant on that answer. Improvising is the ability to approach an encounter with knowledge and skill but also to come empty and open — to empty yourself of knowledge and skill to the degree that your expectations do not prevent you from seeing what is in front of you. The structure of understanding coded in the textbook is vitally important; medicine is informed by statistical and normative research, but in each case that knowledge is being connected with a unique individual, an *n* of one. The physician Eric Cassell, who has written and taught extensively on the art of listening to and talking with patients, reminds us that every medical encounter is a theater piece played out between two or more unique human beings. He points out that conversation and listening are art forms that can be practiced and learned. Even if the standard diagnosis fits, you still have to see *how* it fits into the context of a particular person's life. This is the art of being present: as direct as possible an encounter with the data and experience that come our way. "Listen to the patient," said the physician William Osler. "He is telling you the diagnosis."

. . .

Listening requires no special equipment or prerequisites. What is our experience now? Immediately sounds become present, from all directions. In a city, motor noises are of almost infinite variety. Shouts of children from nearby playgrounds blend with gusts of wind, snatches of conversations, and phone calls of passers-by. We become conscious of culture-as-nature, the city as a complex environment of collective adaptation. The more we are able to hear — including the annoying sounds — the more we are able to take a concerted interest in those sounds, and the more information we have. Then when we improvise, in partnership with another human being, we can pick up the patterns we need, from our continuous cycle of adjustment and response.

There is one prerequisite, at least for me. I have to be quiet. Talking is an effective way to not hear. That is the key in playing music too.

. . .

The simplest way to respond to another person is to imitate, to be simultaneous together. There is no need to be original.

Our attempts to imitate are inevitably colored by our own quirks and proclivities, by the sounds we have heard and liked, by the way each unique body and mind interacts with the instrument and the environment. Attempts at originality will set you drifting off course, while attempts to listen, connect, and respond will reflect your original nature in its ecology of relationship.

• • •

Two musicians stand up to play. Neither knows what the other is about to do. Within a few brief moments, we lock onto a pitch relationship. The relationship may be consonant or dissonant (however those terms are defined by the local culture), mutually reinforcing or moving inversely to each other. During those moments, what are we doing? Fishing for pitches, testing out rhythms and tone colors, in a rapid series of trials and errors. With intense mutual listening, we find each other; then we've established a place from which we can explore many possible relationships: amplifying, challenging, simplifying, elaborating, calling and answering, resting in silence.

Fishing for pitches is recursive feedback, one of the basic life functions, from intracellular systems to ecosystems. We evolve from imitation to conversation to theater. Our interplay is shaped by response and context, becoming more refined and complex. Such is the everyday process of meeting another person and modifying your speech, discovering which words work and which words don't. We blend, clash, bend toward or away from each other in the delicate and exhilarating act of negotiation.

• • •

In 1913 the pioneering American composer Charles Ives subtitled his second string quartet thus: "4 men — who converse, discuss, argue *(in re: 'Politick')*, fight, shake hands, shut up — then walk up the mountainside to view the firmament."

• • •

A door creaks along an invisible hallway to our left, a fly buzzes next to the window on our right, an air duct makes sucking sounds above our heads. All-around three-dimensional sound locates our bodies in the world. Alone, in a crowd, with a friend, in a meeting, in a classroom, or in the classroom that is any spot on earth: we are not simply hearing sounds in all their variety but hearing them in *this* place and time. We are here, nowhere else. These spatialized experiences might be simulated with stereo or surround-sound recordings, but attractive and pleasurable as those technologies are, they are not the same as presence. Sound and silence envelop us, left and right, ahead and behind, but also up and down, reflecting our own body movements, with echoes pinging off walls and other surfaces, each surface with its individual shape and density, depending on where we sit. We don't have nearly the virtuosic echolocation of dolphins, or dogs' ability to smell in stereo. But we can cultivate hints of such gifts.

Listening, we begin to develop a feeling for our exosomatic brain and body, extending toward larger reaches of space and time. Sound is touch at a distance. Awareness of context is a baby step toward wisdom. All events take place surrounded by larger, irreproducible layers of context. Yes, we *know* this, but to *feel* it is a further step in developing consciousness. The uniqueness of every location, of each person or combination of people — this is the raw material of improvising.

• • •

Now I will do nothing but listen,
To accrue what I hear into this song,
to let sounds contribute toward it.
— Walt Whitman

My fingers make little thwacking noises on the keys as I type on my porch in central Virginia. Other sounds arrive from points right, left, above, below, ahead, behind, a hundred feet away, a thousand feet away: cardinal, indigo bunting, ruby-throated hummingbird, dark-eyed junco, grackle, catbird, blue jay, mourning dove, white-breasted nuthatch, scarlet tanager, wren, robin. Distant howl of the freeway to the south. Pileated woodpecker jackhammering up ahead. Crows. Canada geese far above. Eight wild turkeys, running in formation and gacking. The repeated sevenfold wheeps of a pair of tufted titmice, dialoging back and forth across a hundred yards of thick poplar and pine. Their conversation goes on for hours.

Alone, at midnight, one owl. Bats flapping. Stinkbugs, crickets, cicadas. Frogs down in the stream. The mutable, nonarticulated sounds of water — their range, variety, subtlety of ripples and roars captured visually in Leonardo's water drawings.

Trains, three miles away, three times a day, emit industrial sounds resembling rust. In the long sound of the train the pitch rises, then falls, then slowly disintegrates. We hear the Doppler shift, the same pattern that tells us (in variations of the wavelength of light) how fast the stars are receding from each other. Patterns of sound waves and patterns of light waves resemble each other. In synesthesia we feel the color of sound, the touch of sound: all that our enlarged and numerous senses can perceive.

Even if you have the rare experience of sitting in an anechoic chamber, you experience the sounds of your thrumming pulses. There is information everywhere, and we have the capacity to discover the patterns by which that information weaves a world.

A motor grinds outdoors. If it is my lawnmower, I discount the noise, knowing it will go away. If it is someone else's, it's an irritation. There is a profound teaching in the lawnmower: the interaction of thought with raw sensations. It's the same noise, one way or the other. The noise may be a spur to creating music, or an obstacle to it, a poem or an obstacle to a poem, a protest, a legal action, jokes and laughter, an urge to escape, an urge to learn about engine mechanics. George Gershwin, of all people, said, "I frequently hear music in the heart of noise."

• • •

One afternoon I was on Staten Island, in a quiet residential neighborhood, near the top of a hill, looking out over New York Harbor. There was no industry nearby, but I kept hearing a slow, low-pitched rhythm, cresting every two seconds. It sounded like an enormous bellows, a stately *Wough! Wough! Wough!* It went on and on, this driving, relentless crunching clockwork that was impossible to identify. I looked everywhere for its source and suddenly realized that the source was everywhere. I was hearing the aggregate of all the noises of Manhattan, carrying across the water, resolving into a heartbeat.

• • •

But sensory awareness is a mixed blessing. Sounds that might be fascinating at 60 decibels can cause permanent ear damage at 90. Music and sound have been used as weapons by the military, and by torturers. Even restaurant music has been consciously used as psychological warfare against customers: studies show that people under the stress of loud noise will order more drinks, buy more, eat faster, and leave sooner so that more tables can be turned over each evening.

• • •

Like many musicians I am obsessed with microphones. Copious varieties have been invented: ribbon microphones, condenser microphones with large or small diaphragms, dynamic microphones, each imitating an ear with its own peculiar response to different frequencies. I love the intimate, warm sound of the old BBC Coles 4038 ribbon mic, which looks like a black waffle iron. But no matter how good or bad equipment is, much depends on the room, on the microphone's placement in relation to the walls, how near to the sound source it is. Putting that metal ear in a slightly different place gives one a remarkably different sound. Context is everything.

An important characteristic of all audio equipment, telephones, and other communications gear is the signal-to-noise ratio. Every device has a baseline of self-noise, plus the noise of transmission from one device to another. Engineers try to give us the cleanest possible signal. Listeners want to hear more music and less hiss. In a theater, listeners want to hear more of the actors and less of the audience coughing or of the air conditioner's noise. But it is also important to nurture the part of our brain that finds all sounds interesting.

Signal to one person is noise to another. Consider how irritated and mystified Leonard Bernstein was when Glenn Gould took him for a drive around Toronto and made him listen to Petula Clark singing her 1964 pop tune "Downtown," with the volume cranked up full blast. Bernstein, known for his wide range of musical interests, said, "Glenn, how can you stand this noise?"

Signal-to-noise is not an objective quantity. It implies a human decision-making process, separating sensations into two piles: relevant and irrelevant. What is the main course, and what is the intrusion? We want to present the work of art without interruptions. Yet the very mission of art is to be an intrusion into our comfortable certainties. In science, discoveries often arise from the "bad data." Think, for example, of Fleming's discovery of penicillin, when by sheer chance a mold blew in the window and contaminated his petri dishes, and he had the sense not to throw them in the trash. In art it is often the dissonance or so-called ugliness from which the next step in evolution is hatched. We have become more comfortable with understanding that signal and noise, figure and ground, can change places.

• • •

James Joyce's *Ulysses*, possibly the finest novel in the English language, was banned in the United States and England as "obscene, lewd, and lascivious" for the first ten years of its existence. Then came the famous 1933 obscenity trial. Judge John Woolsey's final ruling, lifting the ban in the United States, became the most widely distributed judicial opinion in history. In the midst of that high drama was a remarkable bit of dialogue between the judge and attorney Morris Ernst:

LISTING · 145

"Your honor, while arguing to win this case I thought I was intent only on this book, but frankly, while pleading before you, I've also been thinking about that ring around your tie, how your gown does not fit too well on your shoulders and the picture of John Marshall behind your bench."

Judge Woolsey replied, "I've been worried about the last part of the book, and I have been listening to you as intently as I know how, but I must confess that while listening to you I've been thinking about the Hepplewhite chair behind you."

"That, Judge, is the essence of *Ulysses*."

To become aware of awareness, to listen, see, feel things that we thought we already knew, that is the essence of art. When poetic connection with the everyday can leak, of all places, into a federal courtroom, then there is hope for the world.

• • •

> Ineluctable modality of the visible: at least that if no more, thought through my eyes. Signatures of all things I am here to read, seaspawn and seawrack, the nearing tide, that rusty boot.
> — James Joyce, *Ulysses*

Early this morning I was swallowing my daily dose of dreadful, disheartening news from the *New York Times* website. Endless tales of greed, hate, delusion, and species suicide. Then I became aware of the birds singing, the wind. Here I am in the real world. The intimate interactivity of perception brought back to the present moment, I felt my listening senses stretching out like tentacles. If we had dogs' ears, those wonderful flaps of flesh that can be lifted, turned, raised, and lowered, we might have a more visceral sense of how active listening can be.

As we listen (observe with all senses), we shadow what we hear. Mirror neurons fire when we perform an action and when we observe the action performed by others. Sports fans watching an athletic event exhibit nerve impulses that mirror the muscular movements they are seeing. In conversation, we subvocalize what the other person is saying.

Listening is touching. The hair cells in our inner ears feel the vibrations that move them; it is not a distance sense, not abstract. Seeing is touching. Speaking is touching. Tasting is touching. There is no separating the active and passive modalities of perception. Active listening flowers in the present moment, utilizes all the senses: eye, ear, nose, tongue, body, mind, sense of humor. Such sensitivity is the alpha and omega of all arts, and beyond the arts, of all skilled activity. To do science, listen.

· · ·

Jetsun Milarepa, the great eleventh-century Tibetan poet and saint, is usually depicted holding his cupped hand behind his ear. He is hearing the cries of the world. He is trying to listen more completely and compassionately. But I think there is another dimension: he was a singer who spent his life teaching through improvisational song and poetry. He cups his ear as singers often do, when they want to know if their songs are coming out the way they thought they were. We often think that we're saying one thing when we're really saying another. It is vital to listen to ourselves. That is one of the great functions of art, to reflect back what we are, what we are not, how we appear to others, what we might become.

Being a parent means being told for years, "Dad, you never listen!" Even with those we love most and to whom we pay the most attention, there is infinitely more to learn. Our rich discernment of sounds and other sensations is the gift of being present for each other. Awareness of three and four dimensions means being conscious of multiple perspectives, multiple relationships. As many branches of modern science and philosophy tell us, old ideas of linear thinking, of either-or relationships, of polarities and opposites, simply don't apply in the real world. To experience the world through another person's senses, even a loved one whom we know intimately, is quite a discipline. Even more so with a distant person to whom we do not feel connected.

This chapter is not really about listening to birds. It goes beyond the matter of creating interesting music or art. It is about listening to each other. Through compassionate attentiveness, we might find viable pathways through the *tohu-bohu* of our shared existence. It is vital to *hear* complex relationships, including those inchoate rageful disputes that persist through history, to hear the cries of the world as a bodhisattva might.

Hearing the cries of the world as a bodhisattva might is not an abstract religious idea, but a practical tool to apply to our communities. In response to the trend in American history of far too frequent episodes of police brutality and shootings of people of color, police departments must shift to a model of relational policing — a collaborative practice of listening, conversing, bringing police into a personal relationship with all members of the community — to at least attempt to erase the division between authorities and the

Other. Someday we might create, in some partial way, the city as a space where people can communicate. Otherwise we are doomed to generations of discrimination, cruelty, and bloodshed. Nelson Mandela, Desmond Tutu, and their compatriots in South Africa were able to revisualize the slash mark between oppressor and oppressed as an interface, with the invention of the Truth and Reconciliation Commission — a practical, empirical technique for enabling people to move on from a brutal past. This was magic, in the sense of doing something that seemed impossible. But it involved nothing supernatural, only people listening to each other.

Interruptions and Offers

If you wait for textbook conditions, they will never occur.

— Nelson Mandela

Practicing the electric violin in my basement studio, I was stuck. I kept exploring, touching strings and bow, hoping to find some new, interesting sound but finding nothing. Is it improv if today's improv sounds like my improvs of yesterday and the year before? Am I a fake? I stood there with my instrument, quietly wallowing in these issues. Suddenly, BAM-*BAM*, BAM-*BAM*. Upstairs in the living room my teenage son had put on a loud, irritating punk rock record. The house was shaking. I jumped, actually hopping mad. But in the time it took me to put the violin down, and before I had a chance to stomp upstairs (all the while thinking that he has as much right to musical inspiration as I do), I realized that the music was actually kind of interesting. More than interesting.

Since I had been stuck in doing the same old thing, I decided to play along with the record. If you can't lick 'em, join 'em, and the result was fun and fruitful. The English composer Cornelius Cardew referred to improvising, in Confucian terms, as the Great Learning. Learning to be a better improviser goes hand in hand with learning to be a better human being, because both are contingent on communicating with others, remaining open to surprise.

In theater it is common to talk about improvising as a series of offers. This concept comes from Keith Johnstone, who invited his students to play a game called one-on-one-no-blocking. In the interactive art of improvisational theater, any sentence, word, grunt, gesture, or movement made by one actor is seen as an offer to his or her partner. Actors quickly learn to accept all offers. Blocking an offer stops the action, whether by negating the first actor's gesture, countering with a "better" or cleverer alternative, ignoring the offer, dithering, or flatly refusing. What makes an improvisation flow, and what stops the flow? Johnstone catalogued some of the many ways in which one player can block another. You offer me coffee, and I say, "No, I prefer tea." The air fizzles out of the scene. I may block your offer out of wimpiness, fear of embarrassment, negativity, inattention, a desire to lower the stakes, a desire to appear more skillful than you, or being stuck on my agenda. The forward movement has been tripped up.

In real life I can go out to dinner with you and refuse your offer of coffee because I like tea better; this does not impede the flow of our conversation. I may have a severe food allergy and refuse a dish you offer me. But in the compressed play-space of the stage or studio, things are different: it is more interesting if I gobble up your dish of peanut curry, go into anaphylactic shock, and between loud, gasping breaths, beg for medical expertise, which turns out to be blundering and ineffective. My funeral can be a fantastic, extended musical offering to you and my other partners and, of course, my ghost.

Dan Richter, a superb actor and writer in Berlin, taught a workshop in which he had his students working with physical objects as offers. Improv actors, like musicians, thrive on the intimacies of human interaction, mutual support, and conflict that are carried by language, sound, and action. But what if we see the *thing* in front of us — a book, a table, a rug, a window, a plant — not as a prop we can use or ignore but as an active participant in the moment, presenting an offer of interaction? A powerful idea, especially if you are stuck. Look around you, in a room, in a city, in a forest. Any object will do. As Kurt Vonnegut tells us, "Strange travel suggestions are dancing lessons from God."

What if musicians saw their instruments, or parts of their instruments, as offers — or as living beings who are asking for a favor? A violist searching with muscle consciousness for the balance points of a beautiful bow, a bassoonist salivating over an exquisitely cut reed, a tabla player feeling for the sweet spots of the *bāyāñ*'s skin. Each of us finds instruments fascinating, loving the details of craftsmanship and obsessing over the flaws that we compensate for. Instruments, as visual art objects, as functional sound generators, as tactile and proprioceptive extensions of the body, all at once, can become a bridge between parallel universes. What about extended techniques? My nonmusician son figured out that you can get an interesting sound from a guitar string by gently running an electric toothbrush over it. I've been playing an eighteenth-century viola d'amore with the cardboard tubes left over from rolls of paper towels. Amazing sounds: my favorite timbral discovery of the past few years.

Musicians and dancers who perform in interaction with

visual art know how strongly an inanimate object can behave as an interactive partner, bristling with offers and suggestions. The more we give ourselves over to these offers, the more we are able to give up control, the more we can discover all kinds of riches.

Improvising musicians use sound as an offer. The buzzing of a light fixture, which might ruin a humdrum performance of a great classic, may in improv invite us to interact with a new kind of drone and a new set of overtones. In the middle of a piece we may see this instrument we've been playing with for years, right next to our face, but here's a new detail or asymmetry or flaw we've never noticed before, a new kinesthetic relationship, and suddenly a new direction in the piece opens up. Beyond the instruments there is also the floor, the room, the clock, the beautiful and the annoying things that strike our senses. We don't need to content ourselves with playing *on* the stage; we can play *with* the stage.

Dan's concept of objects as offers really struck home for me. As an improviser and teacher, I love people, and practice a social and extraverted art form of give-and-take with my partners. In my studio I sometimes feel dried up and dumb. But to look around me and see my instrument as an offer, each of its parts as an offer; to see my instrument as an Other, a somewhat alien being with its own desires, is wonderful. Accepting objects as offers — this is why we like to play with toys and technologies. A new tool is an offer of pattern-making possibilities. A bow, a reverb unit, a piece of software that might make a slight difference in tone may wake up a world of response in us. And it might invigorate our interaction with our old tools too. Such are the pleasures of the machine shop or the woodworking garage. Our creativity is like an octopus that delights in wrapping its tentacles around objects of different sizes, shapes, and textures. When writing becomes a morass of confusion, I have learned to see the objects on my desk as offers, and even the desk itself. I am rescued by the mundane object right under my nose. It's never ending. I'm fortunate to be able to interact with these objects, which are nothing special but are precious in the surprises they bring.

And of course there is no better offer than other people: a new person with whom we can converse and co-create or an old relationship refreshed.

Life is a nonstop play of interruptions. We often think of the artist as someone imagining, creating elaborate patterns, but rudely interrupted by the "ordinary" things of daily life. Now that my car repair, shopping, and other errands have taken up much of the day, how will I ever concentrate on my work? That is the time to remember that our ordinary mind *is* the Tao. One night eight of us enjoyed a perfect evening of improvisation, blissful voices, instruments, storytelling, and movement that arose because I ran into one of my partners in the toilet paper aisle of the supermarket and we realized that we hadn't seen each other in months and had to do something about it.

This is the dance of daily interaction with objects. Does that experience push us beyond our expectations? Musicians sometimes learn that their instruments, even if they are beautiful, refined products of an ancient technology, can become as boring as kitchen utensils. That is the negative side of practice. Of course, pots and pans are often our first, and sometimes very beautiful and effective, musical instruments. Everything we are bored by can be reanimated by an instantaneous act of imagination, a shift in perspective.

The coffee maker whines and gurgles — it is time for a

duet of voice and machine. Sing along, imitate, sing against; now turn the three-note noise into a melody that can repeat and evolve long after the coffee maker is shut down.

During a concert we hear a fire siren screeching down the street outside, or an infant screaming in the hall. We might keep playing and let the disturbance subside, or we might let it in and incorporate it. Occasionally those disturbances become welcome coincidences. Some of the best moments I have witnessed in live performances have occurred when the instruments go *pitter*; then there's a pause, and a sudden spurt of rain way up on the skylight goes *patter*. While improvising, we might go yet further and actively incorporate the rain or the siren. During a musical event the siren might become a new voice, a rising and falling glissando that can be imitated by the musicians, repeated, altered, woven into a wailing figure on the double bass over which the saxophone finds a new story to tell. During a theater piece, the siren might prompt an actor in a new direction. Perhaps her rich uncle is being rushed to the hospital, igniting a family feud onstage.

Many of us — musicians, athletes, artists — play with, or in spite of, physical disabilities. We can regard the disability as a barrier or as an offer to which we can respond creatively. The disability has a specific shape and form that can stimulate a compensatory response, a new way of working. Django Reinhardt played the century's most wild gypsy jazz guitar with two fingers paralyzed. Jordon Scott's poetry foregrounds his lifelong stutter and makes it the centerpiece of his work *Blurt*. One of the greatest living drummers, Evelyn Glennie, is deaf. I myself play with a broken arm that has never fully healed. Obstacles are offers.

When we speak of offers, we are really speaking of inspiration. Yehudi Menuhin said, "So they inspire you," when I spoke of improvising music to pieces of abstract visual art or film. He used the same words when we spoke of playing violin or singing with the *tanpura*, the Indian stringed instrument that puts out a continuous drone as a baseline for almost endless improvisation. At the time I found his expression charming and old-fashioned, too quaint, perhaps, for our contemporary ironic ethos, as were many of his words.

As I kneel down on the kitchen floor to scrub off a hunk of gunk, I might view the wet paper towel and the striated slats of hardwood as a bit of trivial drudgery that takes me away from my "real work." Alternatively, housekeeping can be a catalyst for new observations and reflections — the shine of light on wood grain, the beautiful scratch in the floor, an image from memory I haven't seen in years — all stirring slowly together inside me as I scrub. Accept the offer extended by interruptions, and you can't be interrupted.

The ceiling continued to vibrate with the record my son was playing. My house shook, I shook with it, and shimmied upstairs to join the fun and learn something about music.

·

Rubbing

Interesting phenomena occur when two or more rhythmic patterns are combined, and these phenomena illustrate very aptly the enrichment of information that occurs when one description is combined with another.
— Gregory Bateson

One of the most eye-opening things Gregory Bateson ever told me was how he felt when he was writing a draft of *Mind and Nature* in a cabin in British Columbia while listening to a cassette tape of Bach's *Goldberg Variations*. He realized there was an alignment between the structure of the music and the structure of his own body. At that moment he was thinking of his sequence of twenty-four articulated vertebrae, each vertebra different from the others but each a modulation of an underlying pattern. And there was Bach, presenting a theme, then creating a sequence of thirty variations on the theme, then restating the theme at the end. Each variation different yet each related to the underlying pattern.

Bateson proposed that what you recognize in art is that you are a living organism with all the structure and patterning of a living organism. You are, as it were, rubbing the patterning of your organism alongside what you're seeing out there. This is the nature of aesthetics: comparing one form with another, when one of the forms is us. When we feel a visceral connection of body to music, this is it. Walking, dancing, sitting still, our body has patterns, and music has patterns. When they connect, the sensation is remarkable.

• • •

The violin is a sculpted form crafted by a woodworker's hand to complement, be the partner of, a musician's hand. At the same time, that form is made to complement other patterns, the waveforms that arise when you pluck or bow a stretched string.

I rub my fingers up and down one string of the violin. I easily feel small distances and angles — the difference between the part of my fingertip on the string and the part on the fingerboard. I learn things by rubbing that I wouldn't learn otherwise. The sound of a stringed instrument is the rubbing of the strings by the bow hairs, moving at an angle to each other, pushing and pulling on a thin wooden bridge, which vibrates the belly and back of the instrument, pushing and pulling on the surrounding air. Violin playing is made of simple, elemental touch-actions. Playing music, on any instrument, is an art of feeling — you feel an object with your fingers and with all the muscles up and down your body. This is obvious when you say it out loud, but it is not trivial. Singing and speaking, you feel your lungs and throat, back and belly muscles, as you push air out and shape sound — moving-touching-sensing-acting-on, all in one gesture. We feel the feedback of vibrations returning to us, back into fingers, back into skin; a continuous loop. The simplest sensorimotor activity. Protozoa do it.

Rubbing isn't simply physical adjacency, but tactile exploration. It exposes details to our senses that might otherwise go unnoticed. It's the massive gulf between something looking slimy and something feeling slimy. Movement is essential. Rubbing back and forth, up and down, new parts of each surface come into contact with one another. This action can be seen as a talismanic gesture for engagement with art because it can never occur in a vacuum. One thing must be rubbed against another. There is a mutuality in the rubbing of an object not necessarily present in the contemplation of an object. People are said to have mannerisms that rub off on one another. A hand rubbing a tree will leave dead skin cells on the trunk and bark particulate on the flesh of the palm. Rubbing is not a one-way street; it is inherently an exchange of information, a cross-pollination: not addition but multiplication.

We see things at a distance, but in effect we are rubbing our eyes over the world. If our eyes do not move, the unchanging pattern of light causes our retinal pigments to blanch out in a matter of seconds, and the image disappears. The eyes constantly vibrate in saccadic movement so that the contours of the image keep sliding back and forth across the sensitive rods and cones. Vision is not a passive perception but active engagement.

We are interested in dynamic physical contact, discovering comparison and analogy through body movement and direct sensation. As we handle something and *know* it, the sensations we experience come from actively moving in relation to it.

· · ·

Whether it is Jackson Pollock's drippings — the dynamic trace of a man crouching and jumping around a canvas on the floor with a can of paint in his hand — or a rap song or a handmade table, art is, as Bateson put it, form secreted from process. The bodies of living beings, the sounds we make, the artworks we make, are secreted from a process of movement, touch, and interplay, which is life. That is what we're doing, whether we're receiving the art or making the art. Of course creating and receiving are inseparable arcs of the same feedback loop.

· · ·

Akira Kurosawa's great 1950 movie, *Rashomon*, is the story of a rape and murder told by multiple witnesses who all saw, and said, mutually contradictory things. There was no omniscient narrator who knew what really happened but rather a revelation of how the consciousness and the needs of different people produce different realities. It is a matter of multiple points of view intersecting at odd angles. *Rashomon*, in which each person perceives the same outward event differently, is actually the way it is all the time for us.

In large numbers of court cases witnesses say they saw things, but it is proven later that they never saw those things at all. Gordon Allport, the American psychologist, did a study back in the 1940s. He used a tachistoscope, a slide projector that flashes an image for a tiny fraction of a second, to show people a drawing of a subway car in which a well-dressed black man is being mugged by a shabbily dressed white man. Allport flashed this image for a tenth of a second and asked white people what they saw. Most reported seeing a well-dressed white man being attacked by a shabbily dressed black man.

Astronomers discovered, through the Hubble Space Telescope, that Earth has re-seen the same supernova four times over several years, the blaze of light from nine billion years ago magnified as it bent around an intervening cluster of galaxies that acted as a lens, the so-called Einstein Cross. Quadruple images of the supernova explosion were detected in 2014 but also reached Earth in 1964 and 1995, and will reappear again in a few years. The same enormous explosion has been refracted across all those light-years, into multiple images in space and time, each a bit different. Systems thinking, like art, is grounded in multiple views of the world. Our perception of an event — a distant supernova or the story of *Rashomon* — is created in and through context and ever-shifting relationship.

• • •

The poet and scholar Lewis Hyde pointed out that the word *art* comes from the Greek word for *joint*, as in *articulation* or *arthropod*. Thus we have art, artifice, the artisan joining things that had not been linked before, in a flexible, movable joint that has degrees of freedom and play.

• • •

I was with a friend, the violin dealer Jacques Francais, not long before he died of Parkinson's disease. He stood in his kitchen pouring glasses of white wine for us, trembling and barely able to control his hands, his nervous system rusted out from the inside. But he would not let me help him and pour the wine myself. He was attached, to the end, to being a sophisticated and debonair Frenchman. Slowly he lifted the bottle, and clunked its mouth against the edge of the glass to steady it, gently poured, and gradually brought the bottle down to the table, rattling a bit. Smiled. His deliberate movement slowed down and magnified my experience too, as I watched him noticing everything in such detail. An everyday activity dissected into microscopic components, the unconscious made conscious, time extended in this lingering, dilated quality, fractionated like our earthly experience of the Supernova Refsdal.

. . .

Out of three sounds he frame, not a fourth sound, but a star.
Consider it well: each tone of our scale in itself is nought;
It is everywhere in the world — loud, soft, and all is said:
Give it to me to use! I mix it with two in my thought.
— Robert Browning

Find two pieces of window screen, a woven mesh of metal or synthetic fiber. Place them one on top of the other, and wiggle them: you will see complex waves called moiré patterns, forming and re-forming. Moirés look like sound waves; they take on all sorts of organic and shifting shapes. The mind that plays with pattern begins to see metaphor everywhere. A pair of simple geometric grids turns into zebras or waterfalls. The elephant's trunk and my nose are metaphors each for the other. The movement of the painter's hand over the paper reflects internal states, and when we look at that paper we become, to some small extent, a living metaphor for what we learn.

By *pattern* we don't just mean bodily structure; we mean history, experience, instinct, desires, fears, curiosities, which constitute a latticework of being, a unique mesh of junctions and cross sections. Two forms moving across each other generate a third — a new conversation or personality that isn't a product of either self-contained individual but emerges from the engagement between the two.

Two ideas fly together on separate paths and meet in a new matrix of meaning. This is how jokes work. Arthur Koestler captured the importance of interlocking contexts with the word *bisociation*: the explosive little pop that happens when two frames of reference that had previously seemed unconnected come together. Bisociation is the essence of both humor and creativity. Rub two patterns together, and you get a third — or many more. The sexual metaphor is not entirely academic. Yin and yang, the juxtaposing of forms and points of view: that is how genesis takes place. As improvisers we are keenly interested in the moment of contact, the moment of genesis, that occurs every time we touch an instrument, a keyboard, a flower, or the mind of another person.

•

Mushrooms
and Tide Pools

No creature ever falls short of its own completion:
wherever it stands, it does not fail to cover the
ground.

— Dōgen

As a composer, John Cage sought to get the weight of Beethoven and the other past masters off his shoulders. He felt it was essential to be freed from the repetitive patterns of personality and style ("memory, tastes, likes, and dislikes") and to free audiences from their expectations of what art should look and sound like. So he eventually chose to compose music using coin tosses to pick pitches and durations, or throws of the *I Ching*, or other chance operations. I remember visiting him once in his New York apartment, which was filled with dozens of well-tended houseplants and several IBM PCs arrayed on the floor, connected to clacking dot matrix printers, churning out thousands of *I Ching* tosses for a new composition.

Cage told me that he distrusted improvisation because it bears the imprint of one's predilections and habits, and he wanted to create work beyond the control of the ego, to be led into a new experience rather than affirming and reinforcing existing habits. He said that he was not interested in art as self-expression but as self-alteration. I then asked him about mushrooms. Cage was an avid and authoritative mycologist. Part of his extensive collection is now housed at the University of California in Santa Cruz. He got into this field because when he was a student a teacher said to him, John, you are so intent on music; try to be more well-rounded. John went home from this encounter, and in his already trademark fashion looked up *music* in the dictionary and then looked above it on the page. The first word that caught his eye was *mushroom*. Off he went, hunting, classifying, studying, and cooking them. So I asked him that afternoon, as the dot matrix printers clacked away, "John, when you're in the woods picking mushrooms, and you decide which ones to eat and which ones are poisonous, do you throw the *I Ching*, or do you use your knowledge and experience of mushrooms?"

He gave me that broad, beatific grin of his, lighting up the room. "Ah," he said.

• • •

Thirty years later I sit out on my porch on a January morning, gazing at the midwinter sun and the slanting play of light and shadows from the bare trees. A few years ago this would have been a freezing morning, but we live in the age of global warming, so I am enjoying it and trying, for the moment, not to think of the long-term consequences. The thought that pops into my head is: The sun is up so I will go outdoors and write about improvising. The sunrise every morning, the cycle of the year, is the archetype of the regularity of life: predictable clockwork. What could be less improvisational than the Earth's movement around the sun? We think of improvisation as creative, original, surprising. But I return to my daily experience of improvising music — and these improvisations are so much like each other. I have the occasional breakthrough to an extended technique or fresh infusion from another culture. But mostly (and even with new acoustic and electronic toys, with new partners and their diverse personalities) my improvisations sound like me, my dancing looks like me. We live in an art culture that identifies creativity with novelty. We think of creating as making something new that has never been made before, a eureka like the theory of relativity or the *Eroica* Symphony. But often we create more of the same, and that is just what's needed. Beethoven's compositions, through all the phases of his revolutionary inventiveness and spiritual development, sound like Beethoven. The style is the person. The clockwork activity of the Earth rotating, our regular experience of the sun, coupled with the variations of weather and the local ecosystem, physical, chemical, biological, mechanical cycles of activity, all keep producing results that amaze me.

· · ·

With chance operations designed to bypass personal desires, Cage generated a huge output of texts, musical compositions, visual art, and other performances. Yet these distinctively look, sound, and feel like pieces by John Cage. He could not bypass the patterning of his organism. His work is full of his personality and style. Speeches he wrote using aleatory methods still look exactly like John Cage writings. I don't think any of us can escape memories, tastes, likes and dislikes. Ornette Coleman's free jazz opened up limitless possibilities for other musicians, but he always sounded marvelously like himself, and he encouraged us to sound like ourselves as we evolve and learn. Keith Jarrett, one of the most brilliant improvisers on Earth, has recorded and performed solo improvisations on piano for some forty years. He starts from a blank slate each time and jumps into the unknown. He strives every day to develop his improvisations beyond what he had done before, to never repeat a piece he played before so that each concert is a step into a new territory for pianist and audience. Yet his improvisations sound exactly like Keith Jarrett improvisations.

Life replicates as it evolves, evolves as it replicates. The biologist Conrad Waddington coined the term *chreods*, which we can think of as grooves in spacetime, grooves of patterned activity. Heraclitus's river wants to flow in a certain bed, with variations: body, mind, patterns of movement, memory, the epigenesis of cells as they grow. I don't have any cells that existed seven years ago, but new ones keep growing into more or less the same patterns.

There are themes to one's life. Jung called this individuation. As we get older, if we are aging consciously with a sense of personal evolution and learning, we grow and develop, in concert with our companions and our community, but at the same time we are plowing that furrow or chreod that is our personality. As we learn and evolve, we become more distinctly ourselves.

Jane Austen, James Joyce, John Lennon, Georgia O'Keeffe, any creative person we can think of, no matter how prolific, had five or six elements that recombine and interplay in their work and by which we know them. Cage's warm grin was his own and carried his tastes and the imprimatur of his life history.

If you have read Austen and Joyce, they are inside you; if you listen to music, influences from diverse cultures are inside you, digested and assimilated into the integrated complex that is you. Even the music you hate sticks with you, as do advertising jingles and ditties from kindergarten. Likewise with stories, images, films — everything you've seen and known and read can be digested and can become you. Let the influences of your childhood reading and experiences be there. This is why there is no reason to be concerned with originality. Your particular expression of what has gone into you and is now coming out is always already yours: you are the origin.

· · ·

Let us revisit those two old mystery people, grandparents of Western civilization: Heraclitus and Ecclesiastes. Ecclesiastes said there is nothing new under the sun, that every event is a part of cycles that have repeated forever. Heraclitus said you can't step in the same river twice, everything changes, nothing repeats. Both were right. Rub those two perspectives together, like rubbing your hands together. Pattern and change move as a pair, like the foot before and the foot behind in walking.

· · ·

One night I took a walk on a rocky California beach, remembering that I had come to the same place when I was about twelve years old. Back then I was interested in marine biology and dragged my parents there because that piece of coast, from Pacific Grove down to Big Sur, has some of the most beautiful tide pools in the world. Walking down to the shore conjured my childhood fascination with tide pools. They are replete with colorful, wriggly life, close to the dance of evolution. In the history of Earth, the tide pools were the stewpot where life arose, the first Eden. Stepping from one wet rock to another, I became a witness to the ultimate creative process, to the interbeing of the natural world. Crabs and mussels, coral and anemones create little harbors in the rock that fit their own bodies. I saw how each animal and plant adapts its little zone of rock and water, even its very shape, to the presence of the other creatures. They've created *their* space. Community and individuals relate in ever-shifting balance. In the complex ecosystem of the tide pools, every living thing has created a space that fits its own organism in relationship to all the others with which it lives. Over a period of time, which may be one month or millions of years, they mutually adapt so that there is a niche for each creature.

In the Gospel of St. Matthew, Jesus says, "Consider the lilies of the field, how they grow; they toil not, neither do they spin: and yet I say unto you, even Solomon in all his glory was not arrayed like one of these." The plants, the animals, beings in and of their own nature thrive, they eat each other and compete, they coevolve and learn and express their individuality in concert with others. How does nature make space for her burgeoning creativity? The answer that came to me that night, standing out there by the tide pools, was deceptively simple:

*Beings in nature
create space for themselves
by being themselves.*

This image intertwines all the entities that we normally split into categories with our plans and purposes. Form and freedom, habit and novelty, work and play, sacred and secular, are inseparable in the spontaneous flow of life. Questions of self versus community, of self versus environment, questions of new versus old cease to exist. Are we following the path of genetics, culture, personality, and habit, or are we innovating? Expressing ourselves or altering ourselves, or discovering what others have to teach us? These are false dichotomies. We get a taste of this ecological vision in our art that evolves over years and our spontaneous play with each other that arises and disappears.

I take a break from writing and step outside onto the verge of the forest. I find a giant puffball mushroom growing in community with pine, maple, moss, creeping cedar, and ground cover on the moist soil.

Creatures in the tide pools don't create space for themselves by being something other than themselves. They are not concerned about agenda, image, or someone else's idea of how they should act. We can learn something from these simple animals. If you really want to be *this*, whatever expression of your inner nature *this* may be, don't shift over to another place to prove or justify what you are doing. As they evolve and adapt, these creatures are not worrying about whether their activities are innovative or conservative. The vital activities of making a living, of creativity, growth, heritage, sameness, difference, change, are intertwined with the totality of life. It is with the same instinctual vitality that artists should approach their work.

·

What permits us to love one
another and the earth we inhabit is that
we and it are impermanent.   We
obsolesce.   Life's everlasting.
Individuals aren't.   **A mushroom
lasts for only a very short time.   Often I
go in the woods thinking after all these
years I ought finally to be bored with
fungi.   But coming upon just** any
mushroom in good condition, I lose my
mind all over again.   Supreme good
fortune: we're both alive!

— John Cage, *Diary: How to Improve the World
(You Will Only Make Matters Worse)*

Wabi-Sabi

*Is this a paradox? To be in love with the
material world in all its stages of imperfection
and yet to feel that love does not depend upon the
permanence of its images? It is not the images per
se that we adore but the being who lives within
them and will live after the pot is broken.*
— Mary Caroline Richards

In Clint Eastwood's early Western movies, he wears a hat
that looks as if it has been weathered, like the desert rocks,
for centuries. Sun-hardened, faded, creased, and dusty: we
can barely tell if it's a product of nature or culture. The hat
and its dirt have merged into something solid, its brim a battered circle. His character, a grizzled gunslinger, is a man
of few words. But if that hat could talk it would have a lot of
stories to tell.

Among the national treasures of Japan are beautiful clay
pots, which are asymmetrical and slumping, looking worn
and even dilapidated. They reflect the sensibility that came
to be known as *wabi-sabi*. Ideas of wabi-sabi were crystal-
lized by the craftsman and ritualist Sen no Rikyū (1522–1591).
He was the master of the tea ceremony who put together the
pieces of what came to be the traditional Japanese aesthetics in many arts and crafts. Tea ceremony was and is a kind

of performance art, a ritualized interactive duet between host and guest. In sixteenth-century Japan the samurai, the warlords, and the nobility would sit down over the tea ceremony and relate to each other in the rarefied and artistically supercharged atmosphere of the tea room. They used tea utensils that were gorgeous, highly decorated Chinese work in lacquer or gold leaf. The warlord Hideyoshi even built a tea room with walls of gold.

Rikyū became interested in a very different style, a kind of unpretentious, accidental-looking folk pottery that he found around him. He built tea houses that looked like peasants' huts. There was a quality of fitting into the land, beautiful in a simple, rough, and unostentatious style appropriate to nature. Rikyū was interested in craftsmanship that, while reflecting great skill and practice, also reflected Buddhist ideas of impermanence. Such objects put on display the slow evolution from creation to destruction to matter dissolving and reconstituting into other forms.

The essence of wabi-sabi is making something that feels as though it has always been there. The newly glazed pot looks as if it had been sitting out in the woods for centuries, merging with its environment. The piece of music that is only minutes old feels like part of our ancient heritage. Wabi-sabi things feel like part of a natural process.

Wabi-sabi stands in contrast to Platonic ideas of perfection. Through such ideas we came to see the circular form of a teacup as a not-so-perfect rendition of an ideal circle that exists somewhere in the intellectual ethers. A performance of a symphony is judged as a rendition of "the work," which is an abstraction in the form of the notated score. A rock star is often under pressure to perform the song just as she did on the record. A real human form is seen as an imperfect rendition of a godlike or angelic form (or perhaps, today, of "the" human genome). Platonic ideals, pervasive in our culture, lead directly to the modern practice of photoshopping supermodels. How do you fit your real face into a metric of idealized beauty?

• • •

Wabi-sabi is usually linked to visual arts and crafts, material things that reflect impermanence. It is the beauty of the unfinished, the imperfect, the evanescent — even when embodied in objects like pottery or artworks that last a long time. A solid object like a teacup is a verb, the verb *is*. At every moment it enacts its being. Objects may last for centuries, revered as treasures, yet even they are not permanent. Teacups wear down, shatter, become lost in archaeological debris: like a verb, the teacup will cease, in the way that a woman who was running stops running. Nothing material in its makeup will change. Its action of being will change. Imperfection is to be celebrated and enjoyed as you turn the cup over in your hand.

A floorboard or stone staircase is cupped and burnished by years of wear, by the life activity of the people who used it. That stone too is a verb.

Wabi-sabi is intimately related to the improvised arts and the improvised life. The music that attracts me most is sound that may be fresh and experimental but that also seems ancient. Sound that tastes as though experience and life has passed through it. We experience recognition in hearing such music, as though it has been played forever. It carries the inevitability of something you have sensed long ago. Fresh and old, like newly discovered fossils. The archaic and the nascent commingle in unpredictable ways, connecting us through our ancestry. The art is in making something new that feels as though it's always been there. In these experiences we realize the negative space of silence and memory that lies behind and beneath sound.

· · ·

I had lunch with my friend, the poet Gregory Orr. He pulled out his laptop to show me a bug he was encountering in a program. But before he even turned the computer on, what caught my eye was the keyboard, its faded letters, the central keys scalloped like the steps of an old building. A generic manufactured object is worn by millions of touches, rubbing and striking as mind works its way across the mysteries. By the end of its lifetime, the keyboard is no longer a generic object.

· · ·

Damage and wear to an object can reflect how precious it is to us — how much we have used it and continue to maintain it. Each dent is the mark of a distinct story. Our experiences are *in* them, the history of live events, of our adventures and efforts. Clint Eastwood's character, the man with no name, didn't need a new and better hat; this was the one. The musical instrument, the writing implement, the paintbrush that we cannot put down because of how well we know its flaws, will show wear like the scuffing of old shoes that have grown to fit us, and we to fit them. Van Gogh made multiple paintings of battered, worn pairs of shoes, the leather wrinkling up out of space and time to touch us now. Beethoven, also a consummate craftsman, wrote music that captured the out-of-control storm of life rather than mannered and delicate beauty.

Rust makes things beautiful. Rust (one of the meanings of *sabi*) is the relic of a story, the story of something lost, ended, abandoned. A huge amount of art depicts emptied, dilapidated factories, decaying in disuse, that focus our eyes on change and loss. Sometimes we feel most alive when we are most sensitive to pain, when we're touched by stories of grief and transformation. We see in those pictures of decay the desolation of communities, the loss of jobs, the pain of working people with no place to go. We see in the uneven jar the weight of clay dug from the earth, the effort of the laborer, the heart of the lonesome potter (lonesome, one of the meanings of *wabi*), the sensitivity of her fingers running over the bumps of the jar on her wheel.

• • •

A lone rock in a field. A sax blowing once and letting the silence move in.

• • • •

In a park in Geneva is a museum of science history, full of seventeenth- through nineteenth-century apparatus. This was the age when our mathematical and materialistic worldview took firm root, yet each instrument is artistic, individual, not to be replicated. In these lovingly crafted implements of brass and glass, the physical beauty of the instrument goes hand in hand with its intellectual function. It is fascinating to contrast these devices with their modern equivalents. Scientific instrumentation in the twentieth century took a sharp turn toward the strictly utilitarian. An anti-aesthetic bias pervades many fields. Instruments and the spaces where we use them have a practical function, and aesthetics are considered an unnecessary add-on. This is true even in an artistic field like music. In many music departments and conservatories, rehearsal rooms, recording studios, or orchestral practice spaces can be ugly, with clashing colors, garish lighting, crates of equipment piled helter-skelter. It is as though someone were thinking that music is entirely and only about sound, and who cares what the place looks like? And of course hospitals and other medical facilities are notorious for their utilitarian ugliness.

The Arts and Crafts movement of the late nineteenth century reveled in the sensuous utility and much-rubbed artfulness of everyday objects. Figures such as William Morris, John Ruskin, Julia Morgan, and Eric Gill saw the crafted implements of daily life and the home as the answers to the inhumanity of industrial monoculture. Integral to their aesthetic was the view that manual work has dignity. Such a sensibility accepts and enjoys technology without losing the personal and interactive dimension. Here is this piece of wood, what do I desire to do with it? Here is this bit of computer code, what do I desire to do with it? What do we desire to do with these implements and artifacts together, as friends in a room, conversing on a human scale?

· · ·

In 1759 the English poet Edward Young wrote one of the first books on the subject of creativity, *Conjectures on Original Composition*. He wrote,

> *An Original may be said to be of vegetable nature; it rises spontaneously from the vital root of genius; it grows, it is not made.*

In Young's century the word *vegetable* meant what we would today call *biological*. Young goes on to contrast the organic natural arising of imaginative process with work that is deliberately planned and mechanically executed. In some of our conventional ideas of creativity we think of beginning with an outline, an architectural blueprint, and then realizing it. Purposive and linear, this idea is exemplified by the medieval image of God with a pair of compasses designing the universe like an architect or draftsman. But in the organic world, the vegetable world, as Young called it, all the parts grow at once, filling in, interacting, maturing. An embryo or an ecosystem grows continuously and simultaneously in all its members as they participate in interlocking cycles of evolution and decay. Thus, much of our creative life and work grows, not as part of a linear plan that is executed, but with everything sprouting, emerging, intertwining in tandem.

As you sit in a field of plant life, examine each plant, each blade: they all share a genetic pattern, but each is an individual, shaped by the unpredictable vicissitudes of light and moisture, of the animals or humans who have tramped on it. None is a Platonic form. There is no perfect oak from which all the real oaks diverge. Regardless of their shared genome, each is one of a kind.

Wabi-sabi pottery is made of clay but looks like an organism, the product of a living process — as indeed it is. The great Catalan painter Joan Miró said, "I work like a gardener." You plant a variety of seeds here and there, snip here and there, wait, water, fertilize, snip some more, wait some more. The plants grow all together as a system in concert with their environment; they don't grow in a linear sequence, first one, then the next, then the next. Failures feed information into the total process. Editing prose is a similar process, clipping and snipping the text in a thousand little places until it flows without impediment, until it feels like it has always naturally been this way.

Making something new that feels as though it has always been there: this is one of the marks of creativity in art and science. We did not see the pattern yesterday, but today it is obvious — like a tune we first heard only a moment ago, but now we whistle it as though we have always known it. Such activity feels *natural* — a quality that is hard to define, but we detect it when it's present.

• • •

In craft arts, *natural* can be the way the processes of working material, the tool marks, are left apparent instead of being disguised. In improvising music, what *plays* is the material, physical body of the improviser, the physical and sensory relationship to the voices and bodies of partners. Those elements of music and other arts — tradition, mythology, theory, and algorithms derived from standard practices, which are normally seen as quite important — recede into the background for the time being as we experience real, physical presence, the imperfect, untheoretical, unique bodies and minds of the people involved.

Certain violin bows generate a hyper-present, granular tone. Such tone can be beautiful, with more texture to the sound, the feel of hair rubbing on a string. Complex vibration. A sound with a patina of wear, like seeing the weave of the cloth up close, like seeing the grit in the makeup of the clay. The instruments' material qualities are present in the sound, with their idiosyncrasies and their personality. When we hear that, we note that the instrument is an individual, alive, and it touches us in a way different from sounds burnished to virtuosic perfection.

Organic form arises from the material (wood, clay, sound, words, pixels) and from the way the world is. We criticize modern society as being too materialistic (by which we mean obsessed with money), but perhaps it is not materialistic enough, in terms of caring about real materials, palpable objects, craftsmanship. William Carlos Williams said, "No ideas but in things."

• • •

Geometry generates perfection: symmetry, spheres, straight lines, golden rectangles, and spirals. But lines are fuzzed by patina, innocence by experience. Resistance, gravity, centrifugal forces: the Earth, moon, sun are oblate, flattened spheroids. There are no ideal shapes in nature. We get pleasure from the mixture of form and roughness.

Electronic art forms haven't escaped our fascination with the handcrafted. We like images, sounds, craftsmanship, and even industrial products that show some wear and irregularity, some evidence of life. Some people love to do circuit bending, tinkering with electronics to produce funky and unclassifiable musical or video instruments. With great cameras and computers, we can go for high-definition, crisp images, but the flaws, the inexplicable flashes and worms of light, the ghosts, bring life to the image. People shoot video with high-definition digital cameras, then run the footage through a filter to make it look like it was shot on an old Super-8 film camera. Such filters introduce noise or grain into the video signal, to make it look more film-like, to make it look, strangely enough, more "natural."

High-definition video at 24 frames per second is touted to be more film-like or natural-looking than video at 30 frames per second. Why? Because 24 frames per second (the speed of celluloid film) is just below the threshold of perception at which we see separate frames rushing by. Compared to the crisper and more perfect-looking appearance of 30-fps video, 24-fps video has an almost but not quite perceptible smeary quality. Likewise, now that we have moved from audio recording on magnetic tape, which has a similar fuzzy quality, to high-resolution digital recording, many software companies sell effects and filters that will simulate tape, oversaturating certain frequencies and smearing the sound so that we perceive it as "warmer" or more analog or "vintage."

The composer Brian Eno, who has spent a lifetime working with synthesizers, loves letting imperfection leak into electronics through the working of time. In conversation, Jim Aikin feeds back to him, "Instead of having a technician modify your instruments, you've let the process of aging modify them." Eno speaks of "taking the sound out of the realm of the perfect, into the realm of the real."

• • •

There are certain kinds of craftsmanship that you want to be true and clean. You want the joists of your house to fit each other. You want the components of a camera to be perfect so they don't leak light, and lenses without chromatic aberration, allowing you to craft your photos as you wish. But some cameras do leak light. A cheap Soviet-era film camera, the LOMO, was not light tight. Sometimes it produced haloes in strange colors around the fuzzy, glowing images of people — not what was wanted for good vacation photos. LOMOs were later rediscovered by a group of young Austrian students who found potential in the unpredictable, funky imagery. They begin remanufacturing low-tech film cameras of simple construction, often with optical distortions and light splashing unpredictably onto the film. Colorful and sometimes blurry images suggest new conformations of matter. Soon thousands of photographers went out seeking spontaneous transformations of ordinary sights. Here are the ten rules of lomography:

1. Take your LOMO everywhere you go.
2. Use it anytime, day or night.
3. Lomography is not an interference in your life but a part of it.
4. Shoot from the hip.
5. Approach the objects of your lomographic desire as closely as possible.
6. Don't think.
7. Be fast.
8. You don't have to know beforehand what you've captured on film.
9. You don't have to know afterward, either.
10. Don't worry about the rules.

Each camera has some odd characteristics, let's call them flaws, and these flaws interact with the particular context of a photo with its subject and lighting. When the picture is developed — as when a pot comes out of the kiln — surprise! We may have a piece of junk, or we may have a treasured artwork. As we get more experienced at dealing with those systematic flaws, we raise our chances of producing artwork.

Young people who are otherwise deeply invested in the digital age seek out vinyl records, with their warmer analog sound and the imperfection of grooves that can be scratched or smudged. Vinyl is again a viable business long after being killed off by CDs, iPods, and streaming services. And with the genesis of hip-hop, records, the output of the musical production chain, were *inverted* and used as input, as musical instruments, with musicians scratching them on turntables by hand to make old snatches of song into new music.

We are aesthetic animals, not merely utilitarian beings

who just want to get the job done. We like complexity, we like things that allow us to recognize decay and ending and transformation. We like things that feel biological; we don't need to be fed everyone-gets-the-same-dose industrial nutrient. We love to play in the field of unnameable things.

One of the key elements of wabi-sabi is inversion, turning things upside down, everyday objects into priceless art; it is Rikyū enticing the ruthless warlord Hideyoshi, who ruled all of Japan, to take tea in a tiny peasant hut rather than in an ostentatious and perfect teahouse lined with gold leaf.

· · ·

My friend Hanna, who had never heard of wabi-sabi, took one look at the Shigaraki pot pictured on page 174 and instantly *saw* into it. Walking around it, experiencing the play of light and dark, of indefinable colors and bumps, the glaze of ash, she said that it made her comfortable with her — with everyone's — essential imperfection. This was not, for her, a philosophical idea but a physical reaction. One look at an old bumpy pot, and we get comfortable with our own bumps. Light, color, darkness, things that seem insignificant, lead us beyond the world of the designed and perfected.

On the cover of a music magazine is a photo of a great cellist, with the caption, "Still seeking perfection." The cellist is an avid experimenter and artistic explorer, but the editor of the magazine tries to lasso him into the conventional idea that we practice an instrument to attain something called perfection. Perfection meaning what? Where? How? Platonic ideals teach us to fetishize perfect test scores, polished performances, music without mistakes. Musicians sometimes idolize control — of their instrument, of their body, of the desired colors of the sound. Skill and practice are essential to art, yet they will never yield perfection, except in a sanitized world. Musicians can play consciously *with* their own lack of control.

I walked into a store in New York City. A middle-aged Japanese saleswoman came to help me. After I bought what I had come for, we talked for a while, and on a hunch I asked her, "Can you tell me something about wabi-sabi?" Mariko answered that people in Japan feel that wabi-sabi is an essential element of life but no one can define it. Then she defined it. She said, spreading her hands wide, one palm up, one palm down, that wabi-sabi is *balance*. Balance between happy and unhappy. Balance between growing and decaying. Everything changes. She said it has a lot to do with music, because while no one can define wabi-sabi in words, it can be communicated in music.

• • •

Philosophers have said, at least as far back as the Middle Ages, that art should imitate nature in her manner of operation. John Cage got this idea from Ananda Coomaraswamy, who got it from Thomas Aquinas, on back through the deep well of the past. Art need not imitate nature in the sense of appearance but in the way nature functions, the organic process by which patterns accumulate, interconnect, and grow into relationships. Embracing the way nature operates, we find ourselves accepting the offers of the environment, accepting that we are indissoluble from our environment, becoming conscious of each other and everything around us.

Gregory Bateson said that the major problems of the world arise from the difference between the way people think and the way nature thinks. He was interested in how living systems learn and evolve and coevolve, and in how we can live without destroying the system of which we are all part. Nature thinks by evolution and stochastic process, not by scripting and planning. As a biologist hoping to explain something about the workings of nature, Bateson told me: "Do please think in the way nature is thinking to produce the things you want to explain." He tried to think, and to teach people how to think, about life processes without killing them, about nature and culture, learning and evolution, without reducing them to the pre-imposed categories of conventional logic that don't fit the realities of nature. He suggested that art is a way to learn that kind of thinking.

When we watch a skilled improviser or craftswoman work, we enjoy the deft, fluid movements that seem to hide a great deal of learning. Our first reaction is to say, "Wow, she thinks fast." But it is a different kind of thinking: networked synaptic activity without extra time taken up by rumination and judgment. Doing skilled manual labor or playing an instrument is an entryway into thinking as nature thinks. If you ride a bicycle and try to make the activity entirely conscious so that you make each movement deliberately and with planning, you will fall off the bike. This is the difference made by real-time integration of activity through practice. Skilled activity cannot be divided into a series of parts or numbered steps — or if we do so for the sake of explanation, we then have to lose those parts and steps in the flow that makes the activity organic.

•   •   •

Even inorganic nature, as we rub our human consciousness on it, reflects back patterns that feel to us like artistry. People are fascinated by structures that meld a geometrical exactness with the unpredictability of growth and the roughness

of natural process. We enjoy perceiving things from the balance point between structure and unpredictability. That ever-shifting balance point is what we love in music, in art, in the objects with which we surround ourselves.

When the New Horizons space probe reached Pluto in 2015, our human world was able to enjoy brief respites from the hideousness of our earthly news. Amid war, religious fanaticism, and political corruption, we beheld these extraordinary photographs of Pluto. The scientific surprise was the enormous amount of geological activity that had taken place on this seemingly dead world. But Charon, the largest of Pluto's moons, was the aesthetic wonder. Not made, but grown by time, its form is the trace of big forces that twisted it around the equator, the southern half pocked with sharp craters, the northern half smoothed out by more recent geological events or elements that we have yet to understand.

To historians of Asian art, the most quintessential wabi-sabi masterpiece is the Kizaemon tea bowl made in Korea in the sixteenth century as a peasant's rice bowl and then brought to Kyoto, where it came to be regarded as a national treasure. To me, the beauty of that treasured bowl resonates with the beauty of Charon. There is something here — essential to our perceptions of beauty in art, music, poetry but also to our

perceptions of nature — of the balance of symmetrical and asymmetrical, of pattern and irregularity. Pluto has smaller moons that look like formless lumps of rock. Bigger planets look from a distance like spheroids: when we get far enough from Earth to see its entire disk, the difference between Everest and the Grand Canyon is obscured. The smallish moon Charon seems to have just the right ratio of diameter to its lumps, bumps, and craters so that to our human eyes it is pleasingly on the edge between geometry and chaos. Charon is large enough to appear round but small enough that the topographical eccentricities dramatically contrast with the horizon. The equatorial scars and the planet-spanning canyon are the relic of titanic upheavals. It looks like a static object but, like the pot that has been thrown and fired, spattered with a glaze of ash in the kiln, it is all action. After we are sensitized to wabi-sabi and the beauty of things like the Kizaemon tea bowl, that lumpy moon Charon seems just perfect. It looks like a solitary object in space. But its geology shows the marks of intense interactivity. What we see in the seemingly static physical object is the trace of long *experience* — like the Clint Eastwood hat.

Our faces, our bodies, like everything in nature, are kind of symmetrical but not really. How the "kind of" balances against the "not really" is a deep question that stretches across all the arts and sciences. This balancing act is at the core of both skill and perception. When sensing something natural, we feel the patterning and the individuality in equal measure.

In music we have swing, the fingerprint of jazz, yet another of those elements of life that we can immediately perceive but never quite define. Swing is time that, as it flows, is dynamically balancing on the edge between regular rhythm and irregular. Swing passages, if notated at all, are notated as a steady stream of notes, but they are not quite even, not quite syncopated, not anything we can specify. Swing is playing/singing slightly ahead or behind the beat, or shifting the beat toward a very slightly dotted feel (longer and shorter fitting together — we are all familiar with dotted rhythms from our heartbeat). But it is not quite dotted, either. The feeling of the beat is strong but always off-center as it tumbles through time, with a feeling of urgency and flow. It is like walking with a steady gait but galumphing at the same time, with emphasis that shifts and changes.

Here are the famous words of Bubber Miley and Duke Ellington:

> It *DON'T* mean a **THING**
> if it **AIN'T** got that *SWING*.

To sing or even to say these words aloud is to begin swinging yourself. We are taught that clock time (the sixty-second minute, the twenty-four-hour day) is an ultimate reality, and that we are inside it. But in music we can play *with* time, as a friend. Listen to the Indian sarod master Ali Akbar Khan playing the raga *Hemant* — a slow steady pulse, but he is swinging it, in his Indian way. It is another model of swing — on the beat but ahead and behind at the same time.

• • •

Form is secreted by process, like our bodies and the bodies of all organisms — secreted in the sense of biological activity that is autonomic, not deliberate, yet integrated with the entire internal-external communication system of our organism. Form is secreted by experience.

The battered cowboy hat has seen action, conflict, misery, pleasure. It has been dipped into rivers and has traversed blazing deserts. The hat has been rubbed against innumerable experiences, and each has left its trace. It is experienced, like our faces, our encounters with the world literally rubbed across them. Blake gave us *Songs of Innocence and Experience*. The result of living, of having experience, is a kind of learning that Blake called *reorganized innocence*. When we think of wabi-sabi as the swing of craft art, it reaches beyond static things like visual art; it is action. Pottery is turned on a wheel, set in the unpredictability of fire. Music is tuned on a string, blown on a column of air.

The three-hundred-year-old violin shows the patina of wear and use. We love music that has the fresh playfulness of playing-right-now but also the experience of the instrument's having been played a great deal, and the experience of a person who has played a great deal. When a new instrument is antiqued — or blue jeans prefaded — this is a simulation of age, a simulation of experience that never happened. But still we find these imitations attractive because something in us desires that patina of experience. The history may be faked, but it still points to something in ourselves that craves history and story.

The wabi-sabi pot is not a random hunk of clay. The potter practiced and developed skills for years, to make something that looks imperfect. The person who makes that slumping pot has schooled his or her hands to make things that look as if they weren't deliberately made. He or she has practiced, experimented, thrown away many pots. The musician schools his or her hands to make sounds that feel natural, inevitable, as if their imperfection is just what's needed. The essence is not that they aren't perfect; it is that their sound belongs in the world of living things.

· · ·

We find beauty not in the thing itself but in the patterns of shadows, the light and the darkness, that one thing against another creates....Were it not for shadows, there would be no beauty.
— Jun'ichirō Tanizaki,
In Praise of Shadows

On a meandering walk in Reykjavík, Iceland, rain, then a bright rainbow. I followed the rainbow. It shafted straight down to the ground and led me to a cemetery, the Hóla-vallagarður. Most big-city graveyards, especially those full of history, look well tended, the plants clipped, the stones maintained. Here were crooked, moss-covered graves, zig-zag walkways overgrown, but this place was clearly treated as a national treasure. Hólavallagarður graveyard opened my eyes to a special kind of beauty. This cemetery was in the middle of the city, with traffic sounds in the background, but it was a kind of silence and magic unto itself. The old grave-stones look like menhirs — neolithic Celtic standing stones, merged with the biological, covered in lichen and moss, a weed-like riot of colorful plants pushing around them. The place looked a thousand years old, but it has only been there since 1838. Some of the gravestones that looked centuries old, rough, crooked, and worn, were only a few years old. A woman who died in 2004 is marked by an ancient-looking rough stone on which you can barely read the inscription. Making something new that feels old and wild and worn by weather.

The sun stays low in November all day (Sunday bells tolling in the distance), at an otherworldly acute angle. In this place you get a feeling for being on a planet. You feel the Earth's curvature. The moss, the bark of the birch and mountain ash, tangled branches. But there are no native Icelandic trees; they all came from somewhere else, with the Vikings or much later. Complex patterns, biological patterns, link organic and inorganic, build up layers and more layers through growth, decay, and regrowth. This is where culture has turned into nature, or the line between nature and culture is very thin. In many ways, wabi-sabi is the interface between nature and culture.

At certain times and places we can see that interface undulating before our eyes. Nature and culture are intimately part of each other. Usually we employ the devices of civilization to keep them apart, to keep ourselves comfortable and safe. In a place of stasis — an Icelandic gravestone, a Japanese pot — everything is continually morphing. In the graveyard, vegetation overgrows in this wild way, a profusion of new life. It is tended but untamed. The caretakers want to keep it that way. They are letting the leaves and lichens grow; the new trees grow over the grave sites and crowd them out. Death overtakes life and life overgrows death, playing together hand in hand.

to it is hard.

How poignant to have the sense of the consolation that these human touches constitute. One need not but ponder much..coalbury..apparent the motion and man passes in between. One is also honored for the simple pleasure for a

After-Flavor

The temple bell is done.
But the sound keeps ringing
out of the flowers.

                — Bashō

One of the mysteries of improvisation is how to end it. Does it peter out into empty space to reverberate in the silence that follows? Does it rise to a giant climax that bursts time open? Does it gain energy and quicken and then suddenly dissipate like leaves blowing away in an autumn gust? Often we *know* that the right moment to end is upon us.

Is it over, or has it just begun? Our bodies and collective intelligence seem to know how to navigate these patterns — and to know the difference between simply stopping and coming to a true end. There is something about endings where what has just happened begins to echo over our lives after it is done.

I love playing in the intense field of contradiction that arises from such questions. On the one hand, an act of spontaneous creativity appears in the moment and disappears in the moment. On the other, its after-flavor may persist for a very long time. We know as moral beings that our momentary actions have consequences. We know as beings who live in an ecology of nature and culture, of our inner being and our community, that a limited expenditure of energy may have ripple effects that we cannot foresee. And yet it's *only* a gesture, it's *only* a word, it's *only* a piece of music. Vanished. There is no way to resolve this contradiction; we simply have to live it.

Things and events that are perfect may not have the resonance of incomplete things. They may be more beautiful when — imperfect — they suggest something beyond the information given.

Art lives in the after-flavor.

This is one of the differences between art and entertainment. Entertainment is an essential element of a life that is attractive and pleasurable. But when it's over, it's over. Art (if we want to use the word with a certain intensity) suggests something beyond itself. We cannot be finished with it. Something sprouts in our awareness that cannot be contained, that cannot be satisfied by another object, another experience, that sends us on a quest that may last a lifetime.

The after-flavor of long-gone events, friends, teachers, companions, flashes of insight, a piece of paper blowing above a subway vent, our ancestors and our evolutionary past, mingle with the present moment and make the improvised gesture, the present pleasure or pain, today's song, into something worth having and remembering tomorrow. The songs vanish, reappear transformed, blow away again — yet their whisper lingers.

As I look across the room, my eye is caught by the spine of a book I read long ago. I remember the friends I had when

I was reading it, the projects I was working on, and how they evolved or morphed or vanished in the years since. The after-flavor of the book has changed and mingled with other ideas, and here it is, resurfaced. I may not even open the book again, but the resonance of its language hits me in a way it couldn't have when I first read it. It is as though there were a memory smudge on the spine of the book. I see another memory smudge on the book next to it, on the music recording over on the shelf to the left, on the worn leather coat in which I walked around Berlin, on the blue oil lamp that came from an old Sufi friend and accompanied me to the cabin where I began writing *Free Play* in 1983. Events are evanescent — everything changes and dissolves — but their after-flavor lingers, or blows away completely and then mysteriously comes back again in another phase of life.

• • •

In a church in Halberstadt, Germany, an organ was constructed for the purpose of playing John Cage's piece *As SLow aS Possible*. The performance began in 2001 with a "rest" that lasted seventeen months. The first chord was played until 2005. Chord changes and rests will transition every few years, when attendants affix weights to the new keys. The piece will end 639 years later, on September 5, 2640.

• • •

Tibetan monks create a Kalachakra mandala: six or eight feet in diameter, a large, intricate circle of geometrical shapes, letter forms, and buddha images, entirely made of colored sand. The monks grind fine, brightly dyed stone particles onto the design through small funnels, sometimes wearing surgical face masks because their breath might disturb the pattern. The artwork might be completed after weeks of meticulous work while the lama teaches philosophy to the gathered crowd. On the final day the lama cuts the sand mandala across, right and left, up and down; the sand is poured into bags and then poured into a river. A sophisticated ritual form has been created, elaborated, and erased. Then nothing is left behind. Nothing except the after-flavor in our minds. Wiping it out is integral to the process of making it.

Miles Davis said, "Don't play what's there; play what's not there." The music arises from nothing and leaves nothing behind. Disappearance is full of content.

Koans, and many other kinds of tales, do not explain; they suggest. The wabi-sabi pot suggests something, the snatch of spontaneous music suggests something, and you take a journey from there. This is not to say that the beautifully ornate pot, the music that is thoroughly composed and polished like a jewel, cannot also suggest journeys beyond themselves. But too often art is examined and then left behind in its glass case, like a test with the questions already answered. The final chords arrive, the curtain comes down, we applaud, and it's over. What I want, whether I'm in the audience or onstage, is music that reaches into the silence once it is done. Not just the stillness of the vibrating string that slowly comes to rest, but the stillness that continues to reach into our lives after we leave. Sky, still, a column of light, and gone.

·

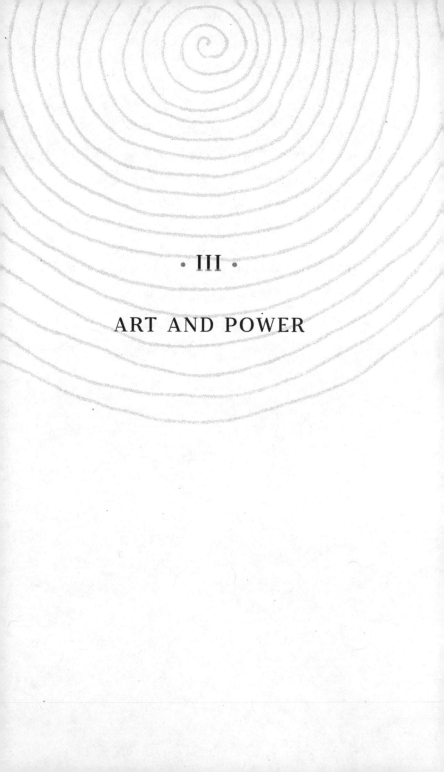

· III ·

ART AND POWER

Cloud of Companions

Glenn Gould was one of the greatest interpreters of Bach, able to play three-, four-, and five-voiced fugues on the piano while keeping each of the simultaneous lines crystal clear, distinct from the others in timbre, touch, and color. His mastery of the independent motion of voices was unparalleled by any other keyboard artist. He also enjoyed eating alone at restaurants and truck stops, eavesdropping on the conversations of ordinary people. He experienced their voices pouring into his ear from all directions, resolving into layers like the lines of a Bach fugue. In the late 1960s he created three masterpieces of spoken-word overdub art for radio, called *The Solitude Trilogy — The Idea of North, The Latecomers,* and *The Quiet in the Land.* In our age of widespread sound art and sampling, we don't know how much we owe to Gould's crazy pioneering exertion. He went to remote Canadian villages, mining camps and timber towns in the north of Ontario,

fishing villages in Newfoundland, isolated tight communities in the Arctic, recording people talking about their lives
and thoughts, about each other. Using the 4-track tape
technology of the time, he blended their speech into three
hour-long fugue-like structures, layering voice on voice
on voice, telling of everyday experience in these isolated
villages, mixed in with Pablo Casals, Janis Joplin, nature
sounds.

The Latecomers talks about love of solitude — but it is
solitude expressed through real human dialogue woven together in a tapestry of community. People talking about their
odd neighbors. Gould's love of solitude and his love of people mixed in his complex and awkward way, through the chorus of polyphonic speech. Even our enjoyment of solitude
gets shared and communicated.

A painter stands alone in her studio. But the acrylic she
applies today was bought yesterday after she argued with
a friend. It is alizarin crimson. Back, back into the past, a
thousand social encounters enter the studio, layers of in-
terlocution in counterpoint. That is how I feel when I play,
speak, write, make a video of synesthetic combinations
of art and music. That is why I am still touched by Bach.
A fugue is a well-defined form with multiple interlocking
voices and a set of rules for how they combine. But often we
use the term *fugue* to gesture toward something more universal. A love song to the interrelated structure of reality.
For many of us, the gift of Bach is feeling the intertwining
layers of sound, sensing the extension of that mingling in
realms beyond music. Or, as in his *Cello Suites*, to experience the virtual polyphony that goes along with the instrument's single voice. Then this musical voice, with perhaps

many pauses and rests around it, flows in answer to an ecology of sounds and silences.

• • •

I am writing alone in a room, yet my teachers are with me. My friends, my parents are in the room, my children, my wife is here. Colleagues, long-gone partners. Someone else's writing sparks my interest, so I read it and find it inspiring. A piece of writing I don't like very much provokes critical thoughts — I want to answer the person who wrote it. So that person is with me too. If a work goads me on to do something of quality, its creator is in the room too. Creation is always collective. Sometimes being by yourself is the easiest way to understand the immense influence of our interface with other people. The writing passes through permutations and revisions, reordering, cutting and snipping, thanks to yet more of these conversations. And finally it is a conversation with you, who may be born after my death. Solitary work and collective work nourish each other, as we negotiate the dynamic interplay of self and other.

My old friend John Seeley, psychiatrist and sociologist, said that the solo practitioner — craftsperson, mathematician, writer, painter, long-distance runner — is surrounded by a cloud of companions. Art arises from relationship and seeks relationship. John said, "There is a love in the nature of things that predates our recognition of it."

What is that love? It is love that erases or at least for a time obscures boundaries. During those moments of free play, we are one. In this postmodern age we find ourselves enmeshed in civil wars, tribal prejudices that we thought we had outgrown long ago. We can dare to counter the spirit of hate and separation with the romantic view of connectedness. I am calling for a new romanticism. At the beginning of the nineteenth century we had Blake and Beethoven and Keats and all those visionaries, striving against the bloodshed and stupidity of a warlike time. That is what I want to evoke in the spirit of this book, a creed of love, people to people, people to nature, across time.

Performing, whether playing music or giving a talk: Is it a matter of being on display and hoping for applause, for good grades or reviews, bidding for approval? Or are we reaching for a deeper connection — that indescribable connection of speaker and listener from which true music arises? We participate in a beautiful complicity of instantaneous feedback. By some indescribable inner movement our brains run in tandem, looping experiences together in one great circuit to create a community of perception.

• • •

In 1956 the great Spanish-Mexican artist Remedios Varo painted *Tres Destinos*: three people sitting alone in second-floor apartments in a surreal city at night. Three isolated destinies that are not isolated at all. Two are writing with quill pens, one is drinking from a flagon and thinking. Dark-red walls. Dark brick streets below. Wispy bright lines of influence connect the three to a star above, and the city below, and their interweaving minds within. Lines of light curve into vortices and converge in space, forming alchemical alembics. A woven vision of these supposedly lone people. A nest of light in a mysterious city.

• • •

> No one knows the end of that progress
> which starts from uniting the perceiver
> and the perceived — the subject and the
> object — into a single universe.
> — Gregory Bateson

How much of what we say and play, how much of what we write, comes directly or indirectly from interactions with other people? Almost all. This is the essence of *ubuntu*: How do we know anything? By being taught by other living beings, in conversation or reading, through experiencing nature and culture, through making mistakes and picking ourselves up and helping one another. *Ubuntu* is the fabric of community, including the community created by the supposedly solitary reader and writer who are bound together.

I have my being through your having your being. *Ubuntu* to our ears may sound like a pleasant idea of oneness and empathy with our fellow human beings. But recognize that *ubuntu* came into prominence as a creative response to the horrific oppression and bloodshed of apartheid South Africa. It is more than merely pleasant to learn that we can listen to each other and build a future together with people whose desires and thought patterns are radically different from ours. To practice love and to create artistic life in response to hate sounds lovely, but it requires a vast patience and discipline. It is one of the toughest lessons life can teach.

·

The Way It's Supposed to Be

DAVID'S MOM: *When your father was here, I used to think, "This was it. This is the way it was always going to be. I had the right house. I had the right car. I had the right life."*
DAVID: *There is no right house. There is no right car...*
DAVID'S MOM: *I'm forty years old. I mean, it's not supposed to be like this.*
DAVID: *It's not supposed to be anything. Hold still.*
DAVID'S MOM: *How'd you get so smart all of a sudden?*
— Gary Ross, *Pleasantville*

What's wrong with reality? A friend is disappointed in love. He tells me, "It didn't turn out like the picture in my head." The power lines alongside the tree-dotted highway slide against the sky like an empty bar of sheet music. "Love," he says, "isn't what I thought it was."

From the car radio, a calm voice reports that the stock of a well-known company "fell sharply today, after failing to meet analysts' expectations." The company is by most definitions successful: profitable, inventive, and a massive employer. But the market treats it as a failure because its actual growth has not matched the projected growth that an analyst forecasted a year ago. Therefore the valuation of the company drops. The company's executives scurry around trying to find ways to convince the market that they are still "innovating" and squeezing more "productivity" out of a business that was already in healthy shape. The performance of the business is secondary to the notated version in the plans and projections. Or if the company exceeds expectations, it sets up new expectations for more and more growth, which will be disappointed in the coming year. On another day, a wholesale drop in markets occurs because "the growth of jobs in July turned out to be disappointing." The disappointment that events had not matched economists' projections overrode the fact that more people actually had jobs. The expectation, an abstract mental model, is considered more real than reality. Experts discuss what it is about reality that fell short. We frown when the numbers drop and smile when they rise. We have an understandable desire to predict and control, to notate events and expect them to follow a script. If only life would cooperate! One expectation that is always disappointed is the unnatural, antibiological belief that a living entity, like a company or the economic activity of people, should be able to keep growing forever at an ever-higher rate of speed.

The radio makes me think of something I wish I had told my friend: sometimes the love that we receive is not the love we wanted. Or once we receive it, it doesn't feel how we imagined it would feel. Sometimes when we express our love to people, they do not react the way we thought they would, or say the words we hoped to hear them say.

This is the career I expected to have. This is the way I expected my nation to progress. This is the friend I expected you to be. This is how a book proposal or business plan should look. This is how a pop song or a concerto should sound. This is the way it's supposed to be...

• • •

How often do we create a piece of art and have it turn out like the picture in our head? Even if we have a blueprint, making that idea work with real materials and real people changes it. And after we have made it, it keeps changing. Words that were fitting and powerful yesterday can fade and decay tomorrow. The same is true of stones, of cathedrals. Finished buildings bend, decay, get destroyed in wars, or restored in new forms. Slowly, and sometimes not so slowly, the continents shift, move, buckle. Most of Earth's landmass was once concentrated in a single continent we call Pangaea. Where is that continent now? In the largest context of the physical universe, thanks to general relativity, which continues to be enriched by new data a century later, we know that the very fabric of spacetime warps and bends. There is no way that anything is supposed to be. There is only the constant mutation of *is*.

·   ·   ·

A revered classical violinist says that she strives to be "the servant of the music" — which she defines as being "the servant of the composer's intentions." She refers to *the* music: a skilled artist acting as a vehicle or conduit for the thoughts and feelings of another artist. But where are the composer's intentions? Supposedly they are encoded in the score. Is it the original manuscript, or the first published edition, or the composer's revised edition? A later artist or scholar's reconstruction? Whose fingering marks and slurs and tempo suggestions made it into which edition? What kinds of instruments do we use — historical or modern — and how do we set them up? The musician has no choice but to put herself into the performance. The performances we most adore, even those of fully scripted classics, reflect the personalities and the collaboration between fellow musicians and their connection with the audience. Each performance of a play, even with the same actors, is a different enactment for a different audience with a somewhat different atmosphere. There is no *the*. If we play Shakespeare, which variorum edition do we use? Do we play *Romeo and Juliet* dressed in ruffs and hosen and codpieces? Do we play it dressed up as modern-day gangbangers? Do we play *A Midsummer Night's Dream* as medieval fairies or space aliens? Which is more realistic?

We speak of *the Bible*, but there is no *the*. There are many versions and translations coming from so many sources, variations of books that have been canonized or rejected, forgotten and found again centuries later. The first books of the Old Testament arose from four textual traditions that were edited and tangled together in the fifth through first centuries BCE: like shuffling four decks of cards into one. Four texts, four styles, four emphases — and four very different gods. The first chapter of Genesis refers to God as *Elohim* — plural. The second chapter refers to the *Lord*, the idea of king or emperor projected onto the cosmos.

• • •

The Old Testament god Yahweh creates people and sets up the rules for their world. A divine score, notated in stone. He is the architect, laying plans, drawing lines, defining the Way It's Supposed to Be. Yet soon enough his creatures start disobeying, with minds and desires of their own. They do not follow the sharp lines of the plan laid out for them but instead behave unpredictably and spontaneously. Design, after all, no matter how thoughtful, is always imperfect. When his creations don't behave as he wished, Yahweh becomes angry, punishes his creatures, wipes them out, and starts over. But they keep disobeying. That is why the Old Testament is so full of smiting. The outline, the plan, the architectural drawing is incessantly grown over by the intricately fuzzy processes of life. Seeking perfection feels tragic, like the cries of Urizen, Blake's gloomy dictator-god, whom he modeled on Yahweh:

I have sought for a joy without pain,
For a solid without fluctuation
Why will you die O Eternals?
Why live in unquenchable burnings?

How can we learn to alter our view so that we accept that we change, go off in unplanned directions, make mistakes? How can we view growth and decay, joy and pain, as part of an indissoluble continuum?

• • •

There is an old Sanskrit word, *dukkha*, which refers to frustration or a feeling of unsatisfactoriness. Buddhists speak of the First Noble Truth, which is sometimes mistranslated into English as "Life is suffering." The original statement is *Upadana panca skandha dukkha*, "Clinging to the five *skandhas* is frustrating." The *skandhas* are the components that make up our physical and mental existence. We cannot be identified with our parts, because our parts keep changing, and their relationship to everyone else's parts keeps changing. Life is not suffering. Clinging to forms that we try to predict and control — "this is how things must be" — *that* is the prescription for suffering. The way reality unfolds can seem so unsatisfactory; desire creates the conditions for its own disappointment. *Dukkha* is the elongation between how things are and the way they're supposed to be. We expect the things to conform to the ideas. Of course that produces disappointment or suffering. How could it not?

To improvise is to act in accordance with what is happening now, with who you are now, with who your companions are. At the same time we realize that this *now* flows within a long sequence of nows. To improvise is to find the pattern in these happenings and develop it into something interesting, without expecting that it will turn out a certain way. Notice that pattern, amplify and share it where possible, and let it go when the time comes.

· · ·

On the cliffs above the sea, in a storm in 1911, Rainer Maria Rilke cried out in his first Duino Elegy:

> *Ah, to whom can we turn*
> *in our need? Not angels, not people,*

and the resourceful animals already know
that we're not especially at home
here in our interpreted world.

Our *interpreted* world: the German word, *gedeuteten*, is variously translated as "interpreted," "ciphered," "the world we've expounded," "our talked-about world." It is how human life, how any life, gets *encoded* from the world of live experience into the world of text, symbols, and grammar. The animals and angels realize that we are not especially at home in the world we have created with our sophisticated languages and technologies. We have coded the world and want it to stick to our notations. Our quest as creative people is to find ways of investigating reality that are not exclusively dependent on those codes and notations. What we are trying to do with our art forms is somehow to use languages to hint at that nonlinguistic plenum that is attained by animals and by Rilke's angels. We can't entirely bring these worlds together, but we can try. That endeavor is the journey of human creativity.

• • •

I remember walking through the immense Parisian museums with my son Greg. In the Musée d'Orsay, crowds of people milled about. Groups of schoolchildren and adults were holding guidebooks. Some even had a printed agenda with check boxes to document that they saw Van Gogh's self-portrait. They hardly looked at the painting itself; staring down, they scratched another check mark in their booklet and moved on. Van Gogh put his pain and joy and wonder on canvases bulging with color. But sometimes we see only the name, the notation, glossing over the reality in favor of the check mark. As Bateson put it, we eat the menu instead of the meal. Let's call it the sin of knowledge — thinking that we know something, but all we know is its name, or its price. Then we become like those financial analysts who see their projections as more real than reality.

Other people stop, captivated by an image. These are people who came not for the sake of a checklist but to really *see*. A couple points out to each other the squiggles of light over the dark water in *Starry Night over the Rhône*. In 2012 their fingers play a few inches above the wiggly reflections of fiery light that played for Van Gogh that night in 1888. Ironically, when Van Gogh was painting, the art world told him that *this* is not how it's supposed to be. He was a pariah. Yet an art lover in the twenty-seventh century may spend a few seconds waving her fingers over the same aged painting of long-gone light. Feel the pleasure of the fingers playing delicately in the space before the precious canvas — of eyes *caring* about light and shadow, senses *caring* about sound and silence. Our act of caring attention to the reality of the paint brings the dead artist into the present mind and the present moment. These interactions have a timeless quality: sinking into the images, one has all the time in the world, with nowhere to go. Blake suggested, "If the Spectator could Enter into these Images in his Imagination approaching them on the Fiery Chariot of his Contemplative Thought..." To accept the offer of the light, to be held by the image and its atmosphere are experiences that cannot be coded, notated, packaged, or predicted.

There is a yearning — poetry and all the arts are full of it — for a kind of innocent undivided wholeness, unobscured by plans and agendas. We cannot define it or prescribe it, but we can hint at it. At certain moments of contact with each other, or artistic bliss, or love and sex, or spiritual ecstasy, or outright prolonged laughter, we get a taste of this state we yearn for, in which we feel we are in tune with what Rilke calls the wisdom of animals and angels. Invitations to step out of the map and onto the rough ground of the territory present themselves to us each moment of every day, like the woman's fingers dancing over Van Gogh's light in the distant future. Right on the edge between music and silence, between words and thought, we can gaze into each other's eyes.

• • •

That was supposed to be the end of the chapter. But four years after the visit to Paris, my then nineteen-year-old son Greg texted me from New York that it was nearly 90 degrees in late October. Same here in Virginia. He wrote, "It's pretty crazy how exponentially worse it gets every year. It wasn't like this at all last year and it was still an unbelievably warm year for New York. It's not this gradually advancing thing at all anymore." We can physically feel that the Earth's atmosphere is sick. Human beings have known for many years that our activities are damaging the global climate, yet we have not responded. Presenting our children with the challenge of living in a biosphere that has been increasingly poisoned — this is not the way it's supposed to be. Presenting our children with a world poisoned by greed, hate, and delusion — this is not the way it's supposed to be. Greg's text intruded on me as I was copyediting this chapter written long before. This may not have been the way the chapter was supposed to end before that text arrived, but it is now. If only we could live like that classical violinist, whose job is to faithfully execute the intentions of her inspired forebears. If only we could live in the fantasies of those financial analysts.

But not one of us has that choice. We live in a world of impermanence, imperfection, and improvisation. We need to do some fast reimagining of what human life can look like and be. Even more important, we need to accept the realities of our situation. The arts, sciences, technologies — formats of human relations and ethics that have carried us this far — need to be constantly reexamined and recalibrated in relation to the context that surrounds us, in this time, in this place.

•

Art and Power

We walk by the power of music
With joy through death's bleak night.
— Mozart/Schikaneder,
The Magic Flute

In the 1990s near the end of his life, I became friends with a
neighbor of mine in Los Angeles, Herbert Zipper. He died at
the age of ninety-three, in 1997. Herbert was a composer and
conductor from Vienna. In his childhood he was dandled on
the knees of Sigmund Freud and was part of the fertile and
intense Viennese/Jewish cultural life in the early part of the
twentieth century. He was on track to become, perhaps, one
of the major orchestral conductors. Then the Anschluss
came, and Hitler marched into Austria. Herbert was thrown
into the concentration camp at Dachau. When I met him he
described to me what it was like, the second or third day of
slave labor. The prisoners were hauling cartloads of cement
and digging ditches, and mourning the loss of everything in
their lives. One night something possessed Herbert to recite
a few verses of poetry by Goethe, and, as he related it, he saw
his fellow prisoners standing a bit straighter and breathing a

bit deeper. Another man who knew the poems began trading lines with him, each reinforcing the other's memory; a crowd gathered and came back for more the next night, and the next. The men on that work crew were not all literate or educated; many had been laborers, farmers, or criminals, but they found some degree of refuge and solace in the poetry. As Zipper later said, "Poetry did its intended work."

After a time Herbert met some fellow musicians among the prisoners and started a clandestine orchestra. He composed pieces that they sang and played on junk instruments made of pieces of wire and wood. The orchestra and their audience were made up of men who knew that most of them were going to die soon. Their daily lives consisted of shoveling mountains of garbage from one place to another, and many of them died buried in it. They were in a place where every possible accoutrement of civilized life had been stripped away, where even their names had been stripped away. But they discovered in music and poetry a way to connect with the life within them.

They held concerts behind the latrines. There would be a fifteen-minute concert, and then another group of prisoners would come in for their turn. They posted sentries to see if the SS was coming so the clandestine musicians could disperse.

To compose, Zipper volunteered for the worst job, latrine duty, because that was the only way he could have solitude during the day. He kept pails of toilet water on hand; if one of the SS guards came, Herbert would slop this shit mixture back onto the floor. There would be a terrible stink, and then he'd start mopping it up again (like Penelope endlessly reweaving her shroud), and the guard would go away.

In that way he bought himself the privacy to compose music in his mind, then wrote it on scraps of propaganda fliers that he pasted together. "Dachau Song," which he wrote with his friend and fellow prisoner the playwright Jura Soyfer, spread by word of mouth to other concentration camps. These songs were remembered as anthems of hope for the creative spirit under duress in those horrific places.

To say that music or poetry kept them alive is an exaggeration. Survival was to a great extent random. But those who survived in this context did so without the mind-eating bitterness that might so easily have dominated the rest of their lives. With the help of their art, they remained sane.

From Dachau Herbert was thrown into Buchenwald, an even deadlier place. Fortunately, it was early 1939, before the war exploded, and his father, who had escaped to London, succeeded in bribing Nazi officials to get him out of there. Herbert made his way to Paris and then London and was immediately offered a job as conductor of the Manila Symphony. So he moved on to the Philippines — as far away from Nazi Germany as one could get — just in time for the Japanese to invade. He ended up in a Japanese prisoner-of-war camp, one of the few people to be imprisoned on both sides of the global war. He eventually escaped, joined the Philippine resistance, and spent the rest of the war working with the underground as a spy for MacArthur's forces. The day that Manila was liberated by the Americans — and by liberation, we mean a thirty-day battle in which the entire city was essentially destroyed and a huge part of the population killed either by the retreating Japanese or in the crossfire — he decided that music was needed again. Many of the Filipino musicians had been scattered, but when the Japanese first invaded, Herbert had arranged for them to bury their instruments in basements out in the countryside and go into hiding, preparing for this moment. He rallied the surviving musicians to come out, retrieved the instruments, marched into General MacArthur's office, and said, "We're going to have a concert." General MacArthur asked, "Where?" Zipper said, "In the bombed-out shell of the Santa Cruz Cathedral." He requisitioned lumber from the army to build a stage and gave a concert of Beethoven's *Eroica* Symphony and Dvorak's *New World* Symphony.

That concert would not have been reviewed in the musical press as one of the finest performances of the *Eroica* from the point of view of technical virtuosity and perfect orchestral playing. The songs Zipper wrote in Dachau were not "great" or innovative music. But the people who participated in those concerts came alive as death nipped at their heels. Art doesn't come as a decorative enhancement to life after you have already built your fortune and your missile defenses. Art is life — the part most worth preserving.

Herbert eventually came to America, where at first he conducted the Brooklyn Philharmonic. He became a staunch advocate for artists in education, launching some of the first programs to bring practitioners into public schools as teachers. As a conductor he was no longer interested in standing at the head of a big institutional symphony; instead he brought orchestral music to inner cities that never had access to it. He moved on to Chicago and finally to Los Angeles, where he lived for the rest of his life, dedicating himself to bringing music to kids in impoverished places there and around the world. Throughout his career in America he served as an ombudsman for the power of the arts to change people's lives for the better. In his eighties he was invited to teach in China and found himself in a hotel in Tiananmen Square just when the army moved in to crush the young demonstrators in 1989. Even in old age, he had a knack for being where the trouble was and not being afraid of it. The other foreign guests left the country immediately, but Herbert stayed because he wanted to see what was going on.

. . .

We have become increasingly used to hearing, especially in the hard languages of money, that the arts are a frill, a decoration, nonessential — or, worse, "content" to be vacuumed up by media and internet companies and "consumed." They only amount, in this utilitarian language, to a hill of beans. I am here to tell you that they amount to a mountain of gold. I am here to tell you that the arts are not frosting on life; they aren't an extra little entertaining piece that you add in when everything else is taken care of. Art is life itself.

In the aftermath of September 11, 2001, in New York City, improvised shrines sprang up on the streets, an explosion of folk art, writing, and music. Poetry was suddenly flying over the internet, and people sent each other artwork and bits of film and pasted things up on the walls of buildings. There was a profound hunger for spiritual connectedness — and the sanity that comes from making and participating in art.

One poem that widely circulated at that time was Auden's "September 1, 1939," from another fateful moment when nationalized hate exploded into massive violence — the day the Nazis started World War II. Amid the horror, Auden spoke of "the Just" exchanging their messages of light, affirming life against the negation and despair that was falling all around them.

The key is the activity of exchange. The core of artistic power is the place between people, where engagement occurs. This mutuality, "dotted everywhere," can be found in the most surprising places. Without even realizing it, people who engage in this commonplace mutuality are doing their part to save the world. To keep it — and by it, we mean each other — sane. It need not take the form of heroics but of ordinary life carried on with some sense of joy and meaning. Playing a game with a stranger. Repairing a house with honest, careful craftsmanship. Writing a line of prose and then crossing it out and writing it again. Singing softly to a dying friend, or a fellow prisoner, or a frightened infant.

As with the "defiant gardens" created by the British under Nazi bombardment during the Blitz, the growth of green things and the growth of human life are most strongly evident when death is starkly in our faces.

Mental and spiritual states can spread, and sanity can be just as contagious as insanity. We must remember the purpose of our work: the arts are a primary means for the transmission of sanity. I mean *arts* very broadly, of course. I include many activities that are not virtuoso expressions of theatrical or musical ability; we engage in many pursuits that would not win prizes and awards, that might be technically flawed and clumsy, but that still carry some spiritual essence of communication about the nature of sanity from person to person.

The first thing that Hitler did was to get rid of the artists or co-opt the ones who could be bought. The first thing that Stalin did was to purge, imprison, or tame the artists. The first thing the Taliban did was to banish the arts and destroy every ancient statue they could find. A whole set of negative efforts go together in these controlling societies — suppression of art, suppression of free speech, and suppression of women's rights. All these things amount to suppressing the voice of human relationship.

Art, which may be beautiful or ugly, heartening or disturbing, can put people in touch with the power of their own viewpoint, the validity of their individuality. When perceptions are sensitized, people are less susceptible to propaganda and advertising. Totalitarian states cannot be easily maintained when you have a profusion of art, when you have free speech, when men and women's voices are heard as equal — precisely because these states rely on people buying into the idea that they are part of a machine, soldiers-workers-consumers-childbearers, and not people. This is why we must pay special attention to attempts at constraining education into narrow "useful" pursuits, movements toward a purely utilitarian conception of life. A country should be more community than machine. Today in America, we see funding to the arts being slashed left and right, its role in schools being reduced, its importance in society being minimized, and its practitioners being told they are useless, powerless. Tyrants would very much like you to believe this.

Stalin spent an enormous amount of energy suppressing Shostakovich, among other composers. This doesn't seem to make sense. Why did the dictator of an enormous continent, with vast armies at his command, controlling gigantic industrial economies, busy himself with a composer of operas and chamber music? Because art is power. Because dictators are afraid of the power within people that art touches and makes conscious. Such opening is contagious. The more we can do to spread the seeds of sanity, the harder it will be for totalitarianism, for repression, for fundamentalism to take root. This is true in spite of the limitations of our individual voices. Most of us can operate only in one small sphere. When Herbert Zipper created his secret orchestra in Dachau, he didn't kill Hitler, he didn't overthrow or pacify the Nazis; the whole war proceeded with tremendous horror and loss of life. But he created a little area of sanity that affected other people, and some of those people who remained sane because of what he did lived on to affect other people, and some of those in turn lived on to affect other people. What we create can have enormous power. It's at the very center of what our society is about, and especially those who work with children have a duty to encourage them to nurture ways to connect with each other. Art is power — it puts people in contact with their own personhood.

• • •

Blake wrote, "God is within, & without! he is even in the depths of Hell!" For Blake, God was the human imagination active in the world. Zipper reciting poems to the other prisoners and bringing music into the depths of hell despite all obstacles: this is a service that we can perform for each other, that Zipper and Goethe and countless other artists performed. Thus the social nature of even solitary acts of art like sitting up alone at night writing poetry. Could Goethe have imagined that his poetry would be tossed around by enslaved men in a concentration camp long after his death? Most of the men in this work crew were doomed, but could they have imagined that their poetic experience and song would reappear to inspire others, as in the 1995 film about Zipper's life, *Never Give Up*? This is the ecology of ideas, as real and powerful as any force in the world.

•

Eighteen and a volunteer
In the Movement,
I was kidnapped at gunpoint
In rural Alabama
And imprisoned
In a solitary cell
In a murderous town.
                              Oddly,
After the beatings and threats,
They let me keep a book of Keats.

I was sick and scared. It seemed
Likely I would die there.

I read his nightingale ode —
How he rose above his woes.

The poem was my ladder:
Rungs and lifts of escape.

I read it at dusk, climbing
With each line.
And I was there with that bird
I could just glimpse
By shinnying up
The bars of my cell:

Mockingbird in the magnolia
Across the moonlit road.

— Gregory Orr

Daughters' Daughters

I look upon myself and other songwriters as links in a long chain. All of us, we're links in a chain. And if we do our job right, there will be many, many links to come.

— Pete Seeger

In the Middle Ages, Christian monks spoke of a demon called Accidie. Accidie is a bit like sloth or apathy but more specific — it is the demon who goes around at midday and whispers in your ear, "It isn't worth doing." What if we were in the position of Herbert Zipper and his fellow slaves in the concentration camps? With our lives ground down and hope for survival increasingly unrealistic, the idea of putting together a band to play in secret would hardly seem worth lifting a finger. Or let us suppose we live on a planet where the very substance of life and its intricate interconnecting balances were threatened by giant industries addicted to greed and shortsighted stupidity. The ecology is already on an accelerating collision course with its own limits; the factors in play are so vast that my little contribution won't make a difference anyway. What would be the point of doing anything at all? Thus whispers the demon Accidie.

The whispering might be as mundane as a voice reminding me that I'm not famous so no one will pay attention to my work anyway. It isn't worth doing. Or the voice reminds me that others have already said it better, others I cannot even hope to emulate, so it isn't worth doing. Why bother printing a small run of intricate poems on thick, toothy paper, bound so as to keep it together for centuries? What would be the point of restoring and maintaining ancient musical instruments so they can speak again and allow new tricks that their makers might not have imagined? And it's so much work to play well, to write well, to speak out when the odds are against you!

We work and play in the presence of ancestors, the mothers and fathers, the teachers, the artists and writers, the people who made the music and the science and the technology on which we rely, the workers who made every tool we use, the people who came to the New World in slave ships in hard bondage, the slaves who built the Pyramids in hard bondage, the singers of tales, the wanderers, the lovers whose stories keep resounding. The stories of mistakes and tragedies are part of us too. Lineages of spiritual teachers wind back into the past. Some are remembered, many are forgotten, and all are part of our organism.

Days before she died, Emily Dickinson wrote of the "audacity of bliss." Try, just as an exercise, to act as though playing well is important, to act as though your ephemeral work will benefit other people — to do the work as though that one minute of musical play can bring bliss to generations of people.

The seas will rise, civilizations will fall; in the midst of all this rapid change it may be hard for us to see ourselves as ancestors. But we step into the role of ancestor the moment we begin to speak, to sing, to draw, to invent, because we are transmitting toward the future. It is hard to imagine people centuries from now looking back on us as ancestors, but that is our job and our reality, as we open our mouths to say a new word, to express a fleeting feeling, to connect with each other, to love each other and give rise to something un-foreseeable.

To act like ancestors in today's world seems irrational. It is an audacious move. It requires a certain gumption, a certain romantic stubbornness. This romantic view is so unrealistic as we look around us and see the very substance of the Earth, and of the civilizations we value, threatened by rapacious commercial and political interests, by the poisons of greed, hate, and delusion. But then I turn my gaze to sites of spiritual and artistic refuge, and realize that they often come from times and places that were dominated by power-hungry warlords. Yet what has lasted is the art, the insights, the practices that reflect the impermanence and imperfection of life, regenerated again and again in new forms.

Arrested

Any object, intensely regarded, may be a gate
of access to the incorruptible eon of the gods.
— James Joyce, *Ulysses*

In my conversations with Herbert Zipper I was struck by his use of the word *interesting*. When he was in the concentration camp at Dachau, surrounded by endless cruelty and desperation, from time to time his eye was caught by something. The momentary flash of sun glinting on a spine of barbed wire. A pencil-ray of light striking a piece of junk paper in the dirt. A birdcall. It would be too romantic, too unrealistic, to call these visionary experiences of hope. Yet something there nourished him; he called it *interesting*. Other people imprisoned in the camps, like the psychiatrist Viktor Frankl, reported similar experiences, which they felt made a difference in their ability to stay sane: seeing some ordinary object in the drab hideousness of the camp recontextualized by light and feeling lifted by it. These experiences of momentary beauty were as fleeting as anything in the universe. But they had some effect, like the random kindness of strangers, like music banged out behind the latrines on improvised instruments, like lines of poetry recited in secret.

In other chapters we have spoken about the importance of the safe space, the sheltered *temenos* in which one is free to work and play, teach and learn, laboratories in which one can experiment without fear of judgment or punishment. But safe spaces do not persist forever. Often they are disrupted by circumstances beyond our control. Then what we need is the capacity to be interested in whatever is around us, even if the context is terrible. The ability to become interested in sensory minutiae even in painful places, to engage the imagination, seems to be a hallmark of those who persist in their creativity.

• • •

That low-key, seemingly bland word, *interesting*, popped up again. When Zipper, in the 1990s, spoke in the present tense of his experience as an elderly man soon to die of lung cancer, my ears pricked up when he said one day how interesting it was to notice the sensations of his cancer. Twenty years earlier, his beloved wife, Trudl, a dancer who had shared his wartime experiences in the Philippines, and everything since, had died of lung cancer. They had both been smokers. He said he found the particular forms and feelings of his suffering *interesting* because they enabled him to understand his wife's experiences more fully. Experiencing a horrible illness, he viewed it as a blessing through which he could become a bit more enlightened.

Zipper used yet another mild-sounding word: *objective*. He said he wanted to be objective about the experience of dying, as he was about his wife's death and the many other deaths he had witnessed. *Objective* did not, to him, mean being cold or set apart; it meant seeing and feeling experience clearly. Objectivity in this sense is like the evenly hovering attention of mindfulness: empathic, connected, compassionate but able to step back from our own emotional reactions and respond with clarity. The philosopher Gurdjieff spoke of cultivating objective experience — objective art, objective consciousness. So did Carl Jung. There was, for Jung, the objective unconscious, revealed in some dreams, myths, artworks. In our daydreams and conscious fantasies, we tend to recycle our usual desires and aversions, the same images, again and again. But sometimes — a gift from the unconscious — the pattern shifts.

Interesting and *objective* sound detached yet enable a profound involvement — detached in that Herbert was able to observe and be focused on the phenomena of his dying, involved in that he was totally present, emotionally and physically, with his experience. This was the same man who had started clandestine orchestras at Dachau, faced down Japanese interrogators in the Philippines, and, in the 1950s, confronted McCarthyite bullies trying to close down academic programs in the United States. His entire life was one of action and involvement, yet the key to his style of action was equanimity.

· · ·

John Cage, a musician about as dissimilar from Herbert Zipper as one could get, also liked to use the word *interesting*. Cage spoke of musical sounds, or of outside noise leaking into a musical setting, as interesting. He explored sounds that arise when we leave ourselves open to surprise, when we reverse our biases of figure and ground, when, for instance, we put erasers, paper clips, screws, and felt weather strip-ping inside a grand piano and play. Cage was one of many modern musicians who found ways to bridge the divide be-tween noise and music. He was cooking, with his idiosyn-cratic brew of Zen ideas, recipes for finding new art forms by standing back and appreciating the surprises. In *4'33"*, Cage's Silent Piece from 1952, the performer sits there and "does" nothing — we have no choice but to take an interest in the breathing of our neighbors, in the bird peeping outside then fluttering away, in the supposedly trivial information all around us, discovering details of the environment and its impact on us that we might not otherwise have suspected. As an older man Cage was interested in continuous and sub-tle sounds that permeate the environment, sounds of which we are often unaware because we regard them as boring. He said that if you are bored by something, and you allow your-self to continue being bored by it for long enough, then you will eventually find yourself interested. This can be a method for shedding some of our predispositions, finding an entry-way into beauty and realization through mundane circum-stances.

Cage tended to use that word *interesting* in a precise way — trying to get us away from the hierarchy of values that we as a culture have set up for ourselves in terms of good music, great music, popular music, classical music, philos-ophy, art, whatever it might be. It is vital to find ways to hear and talk about sound, to make interesting sound, without getting caught in the dead-end question of whether or not we are as good as Beethoven. *Interesting* is neutral, rather cool to the touch, compared with the superlatives we often attach to art, yet in another sense it is open to unsuspected possibilities. "A very interesting sound might occur, but the ego wouldn't even hear it because it didn't fit its notion of likes and dislikes, ideas and feelings."

If we allow ourselves to be attracted by small sounds, they will build into bigger structures. Find one action that is appealing and let that action develop. Let perception expand from that point. Do we want to get caught in the question of whether our music is as good as Bach or Coltrane? Words as good as Shakespeare or Dickinson? Do we see a gnarly old tree and disregard it on the basis of comparison to larger, younger, more supple trees we've seen in the past? Better to enjoy an interesting experience than stop it short with our judgments and expectations.

Music and art are often encumbered by these highly laden words that we like to bandy about. *Beautiful*, *great*, *innovative*, *original*, *profound*, *enlightening*. If we allow ourselves to be intimidated by the prodigious technique of the artists we most admire, we get tied up into knots, a kind of self-strangulation. Then we can't even appreciate those past masters any more, except as markers of status. To locate our own genuine interest makes it possible to proceed, to learn, evolve, and keep on moving.

Interesting is a relational word. It doesn't refer to abstract formulations like *quality* or judgments about a work of art as an independent thing to be evaluated. It refers to the relationship between you or me and a piece of music, a sight on the street, an experience. Likewise, *irritation*, *fright*, *boredom* are not inherent in the experience but a sign of our relationship to the experience. We have the dynamic power to alter our relationship to what we are experiencing at any given moment.

Can we now see *interesting* as a state to cultivate in the more ordinary world of making things, not just in the world of great suffering as Zipper did? Getting out of the concentration camp alive was a matter of luck; getting out alive and sane was something more. Rather than distance ourselves from masters, past or present, by saying, "That's so brilliant; I could never measure up," it is more fruitful to focus on the low-wattage experience of *interesting*. Examine a sensation, a pattern that brings some momentary enjoyment. These simple fascinations open the door to many possibilities. We don't need to make something flawless or even brilliant, just interesting — arousing curiosity, worthy of exploration.

• • •

The midwife Ina May Gaskin said in *Spiritual Midwifery* that a woman in labor can regard her pain as unbearable suffering or she can regard it as interesting. "This is not pain, this is an interesting sensation that requires all of my attention." Pain is sense experience. Suffering is one way we frame experience. We often manufacture extra suffering on top of the pain. We let it make us suffer twice.

To load extra layers of expectation onto things, to find the vicissitudes of life as occasions for suffering, for self-congratulation, for worry or pride, to see one's story as important, is normal — but it doesn't help us. To see them as merely interesting is, paradoxically, to tap into the extraordinary space between attachment and detachment.

• • •

The shadow of the pencil drifts across the desk. The constellation Orion or the lights of the town lie mirrored in a puddle. The wrinkled photo invites our eyes to sink deeper. Spatters of mud multiply the moonlight: mere photons interacting with mind. Leaves blow in tall, whirling spirals in the sunlight.

Eyes widen to allow in more light. Extraordinary experiences of everyday sights liberate our imaginations to discover the unexpected within ourselves. Focused on details, we vibrate in resonance between ordinary and extraordinary: loving the glint of sunlight, feeling a pain, hearing a far-off music, giving birth to a baby, remembering a prison camp, finding the next stage in the mystery of creation.

> *new new maze*
> *the organ of sense*
> *reorganized rules*
> *veiny folded mind prowling the big ring of fluid around the heart.*

— Jack Nachmanovitch

Wonder leads us on, reminds us that there is more and yet more to investigate. We rekindle our desire to persist in learning. We do not shut the door on these investigations by labeling experiences as pleasure or pain, as for us or against us. Opportunities to shift perspective pop out in front of our eyes from time to time, so easy to miss because they seem small, but they can change everything if we have the dexterity to pick them up. Atoms of possibility. These are subjective flashes of mental experience, but as *information* they can have a real effect on our lives.

The improviser's adventure is learning how to get arrested. The world stops for the tiny pulsation of contact. Or rather *we* stop the world, with our arrested attention, our capacity to be interrupted and to find learning in the interruption. People have designed elaborate schemes for how to get arrested. Meditations, rituals, wild dances, a meticulously shot photograph that stops a hummingbird's wings. The first time you hear Stravinsky's *Rite of Spring* live. To allow our-selves to be arrested is of course the root of the scientific method: eyes open to possibility, erasing as much presup-position as possible. One interesting perception leads to the next, through the pathways of an open mind. Then we can test the vision, modulate and refine it. We must be willing to be wrong, to be mistaken, open to revision.

•   •   •

Artistically, we get unstuck by cultivating small sensations. To a paralyzed stroke patient, a small gesture, a finger twitch-ing in tandem with a conscious desire where before there was no movement, is a big deal. I say *big deal* both in the colloquial sense of a matter of importance and in the sense of a bargain. Paralysis in both the creative and social spheres carries with it some conceptual burden, from the factors that say, "We can't do anything, the problems are too big." The enormous stakes that we think of in connection with artistic greatness, or with social change and liberation, can be paralyzing, yet there might be nothing more paralyzing than total freedom. Prisoners in a concentration camp might see a piece of blank paper in the sunny dirt as their one shred of hope, the paraly-sis victim might view renewed motion in their little finger as a great victory, yet too often those of us who are healthy and free are bored, angry, frozen. Whatever we can accomplish, whatever we can salvage, we owe it to ourselves and to our friends to do it. When everything else has been taken away, we take whatever we have and use it. We must try to attain this mind-set while we still have everything. We shouldn't wait until we are trapped — in prison, in our own bodies — to treat the details of life with value and wonder. We are not as powerless as we'd like to believe. We can learn to value every moment of our free and healthy lives with the same interest and importance with which the prisoner regards sunlight on barbed wire.

* * *

Virginia Woolf wrote of Jane Austen and Shakespeare as two artists who arrested her attention because their work came out pure and unalloyed. Whatever their life history, whatever suffering and resentment they had might have informed their work but was fully absorbed. Austen never had the opportunity to marry for love, as her heroines did; she had to hide the manuscript of *Pride and Prejudice* behind a shelf or cover it with a sheet of blotting paper when the door opened so visitors wouldn't catch her in the taboo act of a woman writing a novel. But the humor, the brightness, the clarity and directness of her portrayals of human nature were never marred by bitterness. Her wit was sharpened by disappointment, but there was no nasty edge, no ax to grind. That is the difference between being consumed by your bitter experiences and being interested in them.

* * *

Sixto Rodriguez, a Mexican American singer-songwriter, recorded two albums in 1970–1971. While the few who heard his music found it extraordinary, his albums didn't sell; his musical career fizzled and he returned to Detroit and spent the next quarter century doing demolition, excavation, and other hard labor. Unbeknownst to him, bootleg cassette tapes had made their way to South Africa and Australia, were copied and republished. He became one of the most famous musicians in South Africa. His songs became anthems of the underground, especially for anti-Apartheid whites. Rumored to have been long dead, in South Africa he was considered a bigger star than Elvis or the Rolling Stones. In 1998 South African fans discovered that he was actually alive and brought him to tour. Overnight he went from doing hard labor in Detroit to stepping onstage in Cape Town and playing stadium concerts for thousands of people. Coming home from the tour, he returned to his day job in downtown Detroit. What is astonishing is not just his story but the equanimity with which he stepped from obscurity to celebrity and back to obscurity. Now he has become a celebrity again, but it seems to be all the same to him. When he stepped out onto the stage of his first mass concert in Cape Town, he did not seem a man who needed to adjust to the spotlights; he simply was *there*, as naturally as though it had happened all his life. When he returned home to Detroit, it was as though none of his stardom had ever happened.

In the United States, Rodriguez finally became well-known at age seventy through the film *Searching for Sugar Man*. He was asked by a reporter how it felt to suddenly discover that he was famous. He said it felt good that "they picked up on my stuff." The reporter exploded: "Picked up on your stuff!" — incredulous that a person could be so calm and low-key in the face of going from a nobody to a pop star. There has got to be more to it than that! Rodriguez took to his changes of circumstance with utter equanimity. In our society, whatever our profession, we are conditioned to the difference between being a somebody or being a nobody. Shakespeare's Richard II, the king of England, was arrested and thrown in a dungeon. He agonizes over his imprisonment and humiliating loss of status:

> *But what e'er I be,*
> *Nor I, nor any man that but man is,*
> *With nothing shall be pleas'd, till he be eas'd*
> *With being nothing.*

Here Richard advocates for the acceptance of an impermanent world, without really being able to do so himself. Zipper in Dachau was not worried by his anonymity — he was concerned with what must be done in the moment, for himself and for others. For Rodriquez what mattered was not fame, not money. The simple fact that people "picked up on his stuff" was enough — and even then, he didn't quit his day job. Rodriguez regarded his meteoric rise with the same objectivity with which Zipper endeavored to experience his cancer.

• • •

My favorite Tibetan painting is from late-eighteenth-century Buryatia, in Central Asia. It depicts the Buddha the night before his awakening, attacked by the forces of greed, hate, and delusion. Armies swarm him from all directions, swords and lances drawn. He sits there and smiles back at them. Fearless. Ah, what interesting weapons! As spears and arrows fly toward him, they turn into flowers. Yes, this is a fairy tale, and in the real world weapons don't turn into flowers. The Nazis didn't close Dachau for a song. But what of Nelson Mandela in the horrific prison of Robben Island? There is such a thing as prodigious kindness, which arises from taking an interest in other human beings. In 1990 everyone thought Mandela would get out of prison and the civil war would start, or he would die in prison and the war would start — but instead he sat there making friends with his jailers. And the world turned.

Heart Sword

In medieval Japan there was a woman, Shotaku, the widow of a general who had been killed in battle. After her husband's death she moved to a Zen monastery and became a nun. During the intensive retreat and training week in 1339, she left the meditation hall to walk through the woods to another temple where her teacher held daily interviews with his students. As she was returning late at night, an armed man, attracted by her beauty, jumped out at her, threatening to rape her. The only thing she had with her was a piece of paper in the sleeve of her robe. She rolled up this piece of paper and brandished it at the man like a sword, thrust it at his eyes, her voice letting out a powerful shout of *Katzu!* She did so with such spiritual force and ferocity that he became terrified, dropped his own sword, and ran away.

Here is the koan, our final exam, if you will:

Produce this paper sword, which is the Heart Sword, and prove its actual effect now.

Shotaku was later abbess of a major temple, which for centuries became a sanctuary for abused women. She had one art — to be entirely present. Nowhere else. Zipper in the concentration camp was entirely present. He was not somewhere else, wonderful as that might have been. He was not worried about making a mistake, not worried about making great or even good music. And from that presence he could see what was possible to do in that place and time, with the companions he had, and do it.

That is King putting the prepared speech aside and speaking the dream, after years of teaching people to meet violence with truth-force.

It's only a piece of paper. Roll it up and use it. The woman defeats her attacker with a fake sword. It's just pretend, just a little improvisation with what happens to be up her sleeve at the moment. Produce this paper sword, which is the heart sword, and prove its actual effect now.

•

Acknowledgments

The key to creativity is other people, and I never stop learning this.

At the beginning of 1993 I gave a keynote talk at the Asilomar Conference Center near Monterey, California. As usual, the talk was spontaneous but recorded (we still carried tape machines around then!). I spoke of a walk I had taken by the tide pools the night before and of my insight that our human activities of improvising and creating are related to the interconnectedness of society and of all nature. In the jostling ecology of the tide pools, beings in nature create space for themselves by being themselves. This idea made its way into the chapter called "Mushrooms and Tide Pools." We lived in Los Angeles then, and as I drove south late the next night, with the tape of the lecture in my bag, I remember thinking, This could become a book. My wife, Leslie, was then pregnant with our first son. I am about to become a father in four months, I said to myself; my life is about to change totally, so I'd better get on the stick and write fast.

Little did I then imagine that it would take twenty-five years for the baby to become a man who would be the midwife to the book. The talks and travels and writings accumulated and gradually shaped themselves into a whole. Two years ago I thought it was finally finished. But then my son, the poet Jack Nachmanovitch, took in hand the work of editing this book with me, and it was transformed and clarified to a degree that I could not have anticipated. Jack is a subtle, strong-minded distiller of prose, ruthless and sensitive. Working with him on this book has been one of the sweetest experiences of my life.

Our other son, the artist Gregory Nachmanovitch, provided enormous amounts of feedback and discussion. And this book is richer for the years of walking through museums and going to concerts with him, years of talking about art, music, literature, and little things like the fate of the world.

To my best friend and wife, Dr. Leslie Blackhall, I owe everything. Thanks for thousands of hours of conversations and insights and encouragement and criticism that kept me going and made their way into these pages. And for years of patience and needling me to do this. Her understanding of everything from medical ethics to martial arts to the Buddha dharma to popular culture helped me out of so many dilemmas.

I am grateful for many friends who read and discussed parts of this book as it evolved, Gregory Orr, Larry Livingston, David Lebrun, Chip Tucker, John Ashley Murphy, Jena Leake, Lauren Deutsch; and for decades of conversations with Jerry and Beth Bentley, Nora Bateson, John Seeley, Pauline Oliveros, Deena Metzger, and many others. And thanks to assistants who worked with me over the years, including Maggie Bell, Rebekah Brooks, Jordy Yager, Samantha Lane, Sarah Santos, Matt Wyatt, Steve Plimpton. Thanks also to the many friends and colleagues who invited me to speak or lead workshops at their schools and universities, festivals, and conferences. And thanks to the many students I met and learned from. As an improviser, I find that most of my ideas come to the surface in live interaction with people. Kathy Jackson transcribed many of the talks that became raw material for some of these chapters. And thanks also to the friends and fellow travelers with whom I have had the opportunity to play music and make art, both on stage and off.

In these pages I am still paying forward the debt I owe to my beloved mentor and friend, Gregory Bateson, whose ideas are everywhere in this work. Gregory gave me the lifetime gift of tools for thought that have never failed me. And other mentors from long ago include Yehudi Menuhin, who encouraged me to find my path as a young improviser and urged me to write *Free Play*, Jerome Bruner, Ellen Dorland, Rachel Rosenthal, Ben Berzinsky, and many teachers of both Zen and Tibetan Buddhism from whom I learned so much.

I am grateful to my literary agent, Susan Cohen of Writers House, and for a wonderful collaboration with Executive Editor Jason Gardner, who deftly guided the book through all aspects of publication with energy and sensitivity. I am also grateful for the art design by Tracy Cunningham, book design by Tona Pearce Myers, copy editing by Mimi Kusch, editorial refinements by Kristen Cashman, and the efforts of the entire team at New World Library who made this book a reality.

·

Notes

Epigraphs

Page ix, *Sometimes we blur the distinction between art and life*: John Cage, *Diary: How to Improve the World (You Will Only Make Matters Worse) 1970-71* (Los Angeles: Siglio, 2015), 118.

Page ix, *It takes two to know one*: See Stephen Nachmanovitch, "Gregory Bateson: Old Men Ought to Be Explorers," *CoEvolution Quarterly*, 1980/1982. Later reprinted in *Leonardo* 17, no. 2 (1984). German translations published in *Bevußtseins (R)evolution*, ed. Rudiger Lutz (Julius Beltz Verlag, 1984) and *Pläne für eine menschliche Zukunft* (1988).

Tell Them About the Dream

Page 1, *Seven paragraphs into the speech*: Witnesses who have written about this episode include Clarence Jones, King's speechwriter, the man whose text King put aside, and Ted Kennedy, who against the advice of his family showed up for the march. See Clarence B. Jones and Stuart Connelly, *Behind the Dream: The Making of a Speech That Transformed a Nation* (New York: Palgrave Macmillan, 2011) and Edward M. Kennedy, *True Compass: A Memoir* (New York: Twelve, 2009). Other witnesses who have described this episode include Yolanda Clarke and Drew Henson.

Improvising

Page 11, *I am interested in what happens to people*: Margaret Mead, in *Macy Conference on Group Processes*, ed. Bertram Schaffner (New York: Columbia University Press, 1955), 20–21.

Page 16, *Bimstein found himself facilitating*: Phillip Bimstein, "Composing a Community," *New Political Science* 32 (December 2010), 593–608.

Page 16, *In a 1997 article*, Parade *magazine*: Michael Ryan, "The Man Who Brought Civility Back to Town," *Parade* magazine, November 2, 1997.

Page 18, *Del Close, one of the gurus*: Thanks to Del Close's partner, Charna Halprin, for telling me this story.

Page 21, *The power is not in the words themselves*: Clarence B. Jones and Stuart Connelly, *Behind the Dream: The Making of a Speech That Transformed the Nation* (New York: Palgrave Macmillan, 2011).

Page 21, *Doris Lessing called it*: Doris Lessing, *Re: Colonised Planet 5, Shikasta* (London: Jonathan Cape/New York: Knopf, 1979).

Verbs and Nouns

Page 23, *The spotted hawk swoops by*: Walt Whitman, *Leaves of Grass* (Brooklyn, NY: W. Whitman, 1855), 52.

Page 25, *My mentor, the anthropologist*: The phrase was coined by Bateson's friend and protégé, the mathematician and game designer Anatol Holt, at a 1968 conference that Bateson convened on the roots of the ecological crisis. The conference was chronicled in Mary Catherine Bateson's *Our Own Metaphor: A Personal Account of a Conference on the Effects of Conscious Purpose on Human Adaptation* (New York: Knopf, 1972), 63.

Page 25, *He said, "The fact is, I think I am a verb"*: Ulysses S. Grant, from a note he wrote to his physician Dr. Douglas in the last few days of his life in 1885, preserved in the Grant Papers in the Library of Congress.

Page 26, *R. Buckminster Fuller, riffing on Grant's statement*: R. Buckminster Fuller, *I Seem to Be a Verb* (New York: Bantam Books, 1970).

Page 28, *We should not stamp the name of people's religions*: Augusto Boal, *Games for Actors and Non-actors* (London and New York: Routledge, 1992), 5.

Page 28, *How wide the Gulf & Unpassable!*: William Blake, *Milton* (London: W. Blake, 1804), plate 30.

Page 29, *His reference was to the turkey*: Maury Maverick, "Memorandum from Maury Maverick to Everybody in Smaller War Plants

Corporation," March 24, 1944. The National Archives Catalog. US National Archives and Records Administration. "Subject: Lengthy Memoranda and Gobbledygook Language. Be short and use Plain English." See also Maury Maverick, "The Case Against Gobbledygook," *New York Times Magazine*, May 31, 1944.

Page 32, *He said, "Everything changes"*: David Chadwick, *Crooked Cucumber: The Life and Zen Teaching of Shunryu Suzuki* (New York: Broadway, 1999), xii.

Page 33, *If your mind is empty*: Shunryū Suzuki, *Zen Mind, Beginner's Mind* (Boulder, CO: Weatherhill, 1970), 1.

Knobs and Dials

Page 36, *You kiss by the book*: William Shakespeare, *Romeo and Juliet*, 1595, act 1, scene 5.

Stuck or Sticky

Page 41, *Stuckness shouldn't be avoided*: Robert M. Pirsig, *Zen and the Art of Motorcycle Maintenance: An Inquiry into Values* (New York: William Morrow, 1974), 278ff.

Page 41, *The technique is a very simple one*: Sigmund Freud, "Recommendations for Physicians on the Psychoanalytic Method of Treatment," *Zentralblatt für Psychoanalyse*, bd. 2, 1912. Translation by Joan Riviere, reprinted in *Collected Papers of Sigmund Freud*, vol. 2 (London: Hogarth Press, 1953), 324.

Page 42, *The ability to remain within Mysteries*: Letter from John Keats to George and Tom Keats, December 21 or 27, 1817, in *The Complete Poetical Works and Letters of John Keats*, Cambridge ed. (Houghton Mifflin, 1899), 277.

Page 42, *In* The Interpretation of Dreams: Sigmund Freud, *The Interpretation of Dreams* (*Die Traumdeutung*), Leipzig & Vienna: Franz Deuticke, 1900), trans. James Strachey, in *The Complete Psychological Works of Sigmund Freud*, vol. 4 (*The Standard Edition*) (London: Hogarth Press, 1953), 101–2.

Page 45, *In medicine the most common errors*: Mark L. Graber, Nancy Franklin, and Ruthanna Gordan, "Diagnostic Error in Internal Medicine," *Journal of American Medical Association* 165 (July 11, 2005), 1493–95. John Ely, Lauris Kaldjian, and Donna D'Alessandro, "Diagnostic Errors in Primary Care: Lessons Learned," *Journal of the American Board of Family Medicine*, 2012: 25. See also Jerome Groopman, *How Doctors Think* (New York: Mariner, 2007).

Page 49, *we're left with yesterday's walk*: Rainer Maria Rilke, elegy 1, *Duino Elegies*, 1923. Translation by Gary Miranda (Portland, OR: Tavern Books, 2013), 11.

Page 50, *Following the* Tao Te Ching: Letter to "Green Dragon" Toky Kimura. See Bruce Lee, *Letters of the Dragon*, ed. John Little (North Clarendon, VT: Tuttle, 1998).

Page 50, *Around 1660 Pascal said*: Blaise Pascal, *Pensées* (Paris: Guillaume Desprez, 1670), "Diversion," no. 139.

Page 50, *A recent series of studies showed*: Timothy D. Wilson, David A. Reinhard, Erin C. Westgate, Daniel T. Gilbert, Nicole Ellerbeck, Cheryl Hahn, Casey L. Brown, and Adi Shaked, "Just Think: The Challenges of the Disengaged Mind," *Science* 345 (July 4, 2014): 75–77.

Page 50, *The neurologist Charles Limb recorded*: Gabriel F. Donnay, Summer K. Rankin, Monica Lopez-Gonzalez, Patpong Jiradejvong, and Charles J. Limb, "Neural Substrates of Interactive Musical Improvisation: An fMRI Study of 'Trading Fours' in Jazz," *PLOS One* 9 (February 2014).

Page 51, *When thinking calms down*: William Allaudin Mathieu, *The Listening Book: Discovering Your Own Music* (Boulder, CO: Shambhala, 1991), 22.

Page 52, *F. M. Alexander discovered*: F. Matthias Alexander, *The Use of the Self* (London: Integral Press, 1932).

Finger-Kissing

Page 55, *To me, "good"*: Rachel Rosenthal, *The DbD Experience: Chance Knows What It's Doing!* (London and New York: Routledge, 2010), 46.

Page 59, *When the adults realized what was happening*: Al Wunder, *The Wonder of Improvisation* (Melbourne, Aus.: Wunder, 2006), 123.

Page 62, *Nelson Mandela once said that he wanted*: Interview for the film *Mandela*, directed by Angus Gibson and Jo Menell, Clinica Estetico/Island Pictures, 1996.

Page 63, *Think of William Blake's Nobodaddy*: Blake's Nobodaddy is a contraction of "Nobody's Daddy." In his middle and late illuminated books, Blake renamed Nobodaddy Urizen. This figure, the punishing, fearful sky-god, is the cosmic adversary in virtually all of Blake's work.

Page 65, *In teaching, we are, in Blake's words*: William Blake, *Jerusalem* (London: W. Blake, 1804), plate 11.

This Moment

Page 71, *A continuous present*: Gertrude Stein, "Composition as Explanation," delivered as a lecture to the Cambridge Literary Club and at Oxford University in 1926 and published as a book with the same title later that year (London: Hogarth Press).

Universal Language

Page 74, *When we hear the trill of the thrush*: Ki no Tsurayuki, preface to the *Kokin Wakashū*, published in Japan in 905.

Page 75, *Indeed,* huh *is the most universal word*: Mark Dingemanse, Francisco Torreira, and N. J. Enfield, "Is 'Huh?' a Universal Word? Conversational Infrastructure and the Convergent Evolution of Linguistic Items," *PLOS One* (November 2013). See also Jennifer Schuessler, "The
Syllable Everyone Recognizes," *New York Times*, November 8, 2013.

Bedtime Stories

Page 85, *Return again to the rhythmic recitations*: Marcel Jousse, *Les compositeurs oraux*, in *Le Style oral rhythmique et mnémotechnique chez les Verbo-moteurs* (Paris: Gabriel Beauchesne, 1925). Translation by the author.

Page 88, *After Parry's death*: Albert B. Lord, *The Singer of Tales* (Cambridge, MA: Harvard University Press, 1960).

Page 89, *They were using music*: For sources and references regarding these oral poetic traditions, see the books listed under Further Reading by Ruth Finnegan, Albert Lord, Walter Ong, and John Miles Foley, as well as the journal *Oral Tradition*.

Page 92, *Adams then rapped out*: Henry Fielding, *The Adventures of Joseph Andrews* (London: A. Millar, 1742), chap. 2.

Page 95, *One of Homer's epithets for Odysseus*: See, among other translations, Robert Fitzgerald (New York: Doubleday, 1961), book 14, line 213, as well as book 19, line 284; and Robert Fagles (New York: Viking, 1997), book 19, line 185.

Page 97, *The linguist Deborah Tannen suggested*: See Deborah Tannen, "The Myth of Orality and Literacy," in *Linguistics and Literacy*, ed. William Frawley (New York: Plenum, 1982) and Tannen, "The Oral/Literate Continuum in Discourse," in *Spoken and Written Language*, ed. Deborah Tannen (Oxford University Press, 1989).

Page 99, *And so it was that among the gentiles*: St. Thomas Aquinas, *Summa Theologica*, book 3, question 42, article 4, "Whether Christ Should Have Committed His Doctrine to Writing," 1265/1274. Translated by the Fathers of the English Dominican Province (London: Thomas Baker, 1911). Aquinas goes on to say that the teachings, "the law of the spirit of life, had to be written not with ink but with the Spirit of the living God; not in tables of stone, but in the fleshly tables of the heart."

Page 100, *Enlightening mentors*: Thomas Cleary, *The Flower Ornament Sutra: A Translation of the Avatamsaka Sutra*, vol. 1, trans. Thomas Cleary (Boulder, CO: Shambhala, 1984), 57.

Page 101, *The dharma*: The word *dharma* has a dual meaning. It refers to the Buddhist teachings, in their many forms, and to the reality of the universe.

Natural History

Page 105, *When you try to pick out anything by itself*: John Muir, *My First Summer in the Sierra* (Boston: Houghton Mifflin, 1911), chap. 6.

Page 106, *Thich Nhat Hanh substitutes*: In 1966, in Vietnam, Thich Nhat Hanh founded the Tiep Hien Order or the Order of Interbeing, when the Vietnam War was escalating and Buddhist teachings were desperately needed in the context of the hatred, violence, and divisiveness enveloping his country. See Thich Nhat Hanh, *Interbeing* (Berkeley, CA: Parallax, 1987).

Page 107, *For a thousand years they wait for him*: Hsi K'ang: *Poetical Essay on the Lute*, trans. Robert van Gulik (Tokyo: Sophia University, Monumenta Nipponica Monograph, 1941), 74.

All About Frogs

Page 112, *One of the seminal papers that came out*: J.Y. Lettvin, H.R. Maturana, W.S. McCulloch, and W.H. Pitts, "What the Frog's Eye Tells the Frog's Brain," *Proceedings of the Institute of Radio Engineers* 47, no. 11 (1959). Reprinted in Warren S. McCulloch, *Embodiments of Mind*

(Cambridge, MA: MIT Press, 1965). See also H. R. Maturana, J. Y. Lettvin, W. S. McCulloch, and W. H. Pitts, "How Seen Movement Appears in the Frog's Optic Nerve," *Federation Proceedings* 18, no. 1 (1959).

Page 115, *Old pond*: Matsuo Bashō, in *Nozarashi kikō (Account of Exposure to the Fields)*, 1686. Distilled by the author from multiple translations, including ones by Conrad Hyers, R. H. Blythe, Alan Watts, and others.

Page 116, *The Great Way is not difficult*: Seng-Ts'an, *Hsin Hsin Ming*, seventh century, trans. Richard B. Clarke (Buffalo, NY: White Pine Press, 2001). Reprinted by permission of White Pine Press.

Page 118, *To the eyes of a miser*: William Blake, Letter to Dr. J. Trusler, August 23, 1799. In the Blake collection at the British Library.

Page 119, *There is nothing either bad or good*: William Shakespeare, *Hamlet*, 1601, act 2, scene 2.

Page 121, *Of course, there is a real need for thought*: David Bohm, "The Art of Perceiving Movement," 1971; reprinted in David Bohm, *On Creativity* (London and New York: Routledge, 1998).

Page 123, *Can you become a little child?*: Chuang Tzu, *The Sacred Books of China: The Texts of Taoism*, trans. James Legge (Oxford: Clarendon, 1891), book 23, part 3, paragraph 5.

Page 124, *The Sengai frog painting we examined*: Sengai's inscription says: "If a man becomes a Buddha by practicing zazen . . . a frog though I am, I should have been one long ago."

Page 125, *The great ninth-century Zen master*: Mumon Ekai, *Mumonkan (The Gateless Gate*, 1229), koan 19, trans. R. H. Blyth, *Zen and Zen Classics Vol 4, the Mumonkan* (Tokyo: Hokuseido Press, 1966), 147.

Twists and Turns

Page 127, *Unpremeditated music is the true gauge*: Henry David Thoreau, journal entry, August 18, 1841, in *The Writings of Henry David Thoreau*, vol. 7 (Boston: Houghton Mifflin, 1893).

Page 128, *As a teenager Freud was influenced*: Ludwig Börne, "The Art of Becoming an Original Writer in Three Days," essay originally published in Frankfurt in 1823. For a source see Ernest Jones, *The Life and Work of Sigmund Freud* (London: Hogarth Press, 1955), chap. 11.

Page 129, *Methought I was enamored of an ass*: Shakespeare, *A Midsummer Night's Dream*, 1596, act 4, scene 1.

Page 129, *"I come," Blake wrote*: William Blake, *Milton* (London: W. Blake, 1804), plate 40.

Page 130, *Our age is seeking a new spring of life*: Carl Jung, *Collected Papers on Analytical Psychology*, ed. Constance Long (London: Baillière, Tindall and Cox, 1917), 444.

Page 130, *The patient can make himself*: Carl Jung, "The Aims of Psychotherapy" (1929), in *Collected Works of C. G. Jung* (trans. R. F. C. Hull, Pantheon, 1954), *Volume 16: Practice of Psychotherapy*, par. 106.

Page 130, *In his own life Jung practiced this method*: Jung formulated the practice of active imagination in a paper he wrote while on military duty in World War I, in 1916, "The Transcendent Function." It was not published until 1957 (*Collected Works*, vol. 8, pars. 131–93). In its forty years of being unpublished, it had a remarkable effect, generating and nurturing expressive arts therapies in many forms.

Page 132, *I give you the end of a golden string*: William Blake, *Jerusalem* (London: W. Blake, 1804), plate 77.

Page 133, *In ancient times people described certain experiences*: Julian Jaynes, *The Origin of Consciousness in the Breakdown of the Bicameral Mind* (Boston: Houghton Mifflin, 1976).

Listening

Page 136, *Take a walk at night*: Pauline Oliveros, *Sonic Meditations* (Sharon, VT: Smith Publications, 1974).

Page 137, *The average was eighteen seconds*: H. B. Beckman and R. M. Frankel, "The Effect of Physician Behavior on the Collection of Data," *Annals of Internal Medicine* 101 (Nov. 1, 1984): 692–96.

Page 138, *Even if the standard diagnosis fits*: Eric J. Cassell, *Talking with Patients: The Theory of Doctor-Patient Communication* (Cambridge, MA: MIT Press), 1985.

Page 141, *Now I will do nothing but listen*: Walt Whitman, *Leaves of Grass* (Brooklyn, NY: W. Whitman, 1855).

Page 142, *George Gershwin, of all people*: George Gershwin, letter to Isaac Goldberg, in Joan Peyser, *The Memory of All That: The Life of George Gershwin* (New York: Simon & Schuster, 1993), 80.

Page 143, *Even restaurant music has been consciously used*: On the weaponization of sound, see Cara Buckley, "Working or Playing Indoors, New Yorkers Face an Unabated Roar," *New York Times*, July 19, 2012.

Page 143, *Consider how irritated and mystified Leonard Bernstein was*: Otto Friedrich, *Glenn Gould: A Life and Variations* (New York: Vintage, 1989), 176–77.

Page 144, *Your honor, while arguing to win this case*: Morris L. Ernst, "Reflections on the Ulysses Trial and Censorship," *James Joyce Quarterly* 3 (Fall 1965), 3–11.

Page 145, *Ineluctable modality of the visible*: James Joyce, *Ulysses* (Paris: Shakespeare and Company, 1922), episode 3.

Interruptions and Offers

Page 149, *If you wait for textbook conditions*: Nelson Mandela, *Long Walk to Freedom: The Autobiography of Nelson Mandela* (New York: Little, Brown, 1994), 271.

Page 151, *Strange travel suggestions*: Kurt Vonnegut, *Cat's Cradle* (New York: Holt, Rinehart & Winston, 1963).

Rubbing

Page 156, *Interesting phenomena occur*: Gregory Bateson, *Mind and Nature* (New York: Dutton, 1979), 79.

Page 160, *The poet and scholar Lewis Hyde pointed out*: Lewis Hyde, *Trickster Makes This World: Mischief, Myth, and Art* (New York: Farrar, Straus and Giroux), 1998.

Page 161, *Out of three sounds he frame, not a fourth sound*: Robert Browning, "Abt Vogler," in *Dramatis Personae* (London: Chapman and Hall, 1864).

Page 162, *Arthur Koestler captured the importance*: Arthur Koestler, *The Act of Creation* (New York: Macmillan, 1964).

Mushrooms and Tide Pools

Page 163, *No creature ever falls short*: Eihei Dōgen, *300 Koans (Shinzi Shōbō-genzō, True Dharma Eye)*, compiled by Dōgen in 1223–1227, trans. Kazuaki Tanahashi and John Daido Loori (Boulder, CO: Shambhala, 2005), koans 14, 21, 142.

Page 168, *In the Gospel of St. Matthew, Jesus says*: Matthew 6:28, King James Version.

Page 171, *What permits us to love one another and the earth*: John Cage, *Diary: How to Improve the World (You Will Only Make Matters Worse) 1969* (Los Angeles: Siglio, 2015), 94.

Wabi-Sabi

Page 172, *Is this a paradox?*: Mary Caroline Richards, *Centering in Pottery, Poetry and the Person* (Middletown, CT: Wesleyan University Press, 1962), 29.

Page 178, *An Original may be said*: Edward Young, *Conjectures on Original Composition* (London: A. Millar, 1759).

Page 179, *The great Catalan painter*: See Joan Miró, *I Work Like a Gardener*. Published in an edition of seventy-five copies in 1958 and reprinted by Princeton Architectural Press in 2017.

Page 181, *William Carlos Williams said*: William Carlos Williams, "Paterson," *Quarterly Review of Literature* 6, no. 1 (1927).

Page 182, *In conversation, Jim Aikin*: Brian Eno, interview with Jim Aikin, *Keyboard* (July 1981), 62.

Page 182, *Here are the ten rules of lomography*: Lomographic Society International, Vienna, Austria. See www.lomography.com

Page 185, *John Cage got this idea from Ananda Coomaraswamy*: See Thomas Aquinas, *Summa Theologica I–II*, question 57, article 3c. See also Umberto Eco, *The Aesthetics of Thomas Aquinas*, trans. Hugh Bredin (Cambridge, MA: Harvard, 1988), first published in 1970 in Milan; and You Nakai, "How to Imitate Nature in Her Manner of Operation: Between What John Cage Did and What He Said," *Perspectives in New Music* 52 (Fall 2014).

Page 189, *Here are the famous words of Bubber Miley and Duke Ellington*: Bubber Miley and Duke Ellington, "It Don't Mean a Thing (If It Ain't Got That Swing)," Mills Music, 1932. Among the many recordings, an outstanding one is Duke Ellington and Louis Armstrong, *The Great Summit: The Master Takes*, Blue Note, recorded in New.York, April 3–4, 1961.

Page 191, *We find beauty not in the thing itself*: Jun'ichirō Tanizaki, *In Praise of Shadows* (Sedgwick, ME: Leete's Island Books, 1977), 30.

After-Flavor

Page 194, *The temple bell is done*: Matsuo Bashō, *Oku no Hosomichi (The Narrow Road to the Interior)*, Japan, 1694. Adaptation by author.

Page 197, *Don't play what's there*: Miles Davis, *Spin* magazine (December 1990), 30.

Cloud of Companions

Page 205, *No one knows the end of that progress*: Gregory Bateson, "Last Lecture," Institute of Contemporary Arts, London, 1979. Reprinted in *A Sacred Unity: Further Steps to an Ecology of Mind*, ed. Rodney E. Donaldson (New York: Cornelia & Michael Bessie, 1991).

The Way It's Supposed to Be

Page 206, *When your father was here, I used to think*: *Pleasantville*, written and directed by Gary Ross, Larger Than Life Productions and New Line Cinema, 1998.

Page 210, *I have sought for a joy without pain*: William Blake, *The First Book of Urizen* (London: W. Blake, 1794).

Page 211, *The original statement is* Upadana: See Reb Anderson, "The Five Skandhas," in *Warm Smiles from Cold Mountains: Dharma Talks on Zen Meditation* (Berkeley, CA: Rodmell Press, 1999), 35–46.

Page 211, *Ah, to whom can we turn*: Rainer Maria Rilke, *Duino Elegies* (*Duineser Elegien*) (Berlin: Insel Verlag, 1923). Adaptation by the author.

Page 213, *Blake suggested, "If the Spectator could Enter*: William Blake, *Descriptive Catalog* to *A Vision of the Last Judgment* (London, W. Blake, 1810).

Art and Power

Page 216, *We walk by the power of music*: Wolfgang Amadeus Mozart and Emanuel Schikaneder, *Die Zauberflöte (The Magic Flute)*, act 2, scene 8.

Page 220, *The other foreign guests left the country*: For more about Herbert Zipper's story, see the book by Paul Cummins, *Dachau Song: The Twentieth-Century Odyssey of Herbert Zipper* (New York: Peter Lang, 1992), and the film written and directed by Terry Sanders, *Never Give Up*, produced by Sanders and Freida Lee Mock, American Film Foundation, 1996.

Page 220, *One poem that widely circulated at that time*: W. H. Auden, "September 1, 1939," in *Another Time* (New York: Random House, 1940).

Page 223, *Blake wrote, "God is within*: William Blake, *Jerusalem* (London: W. Blake, 1804), plate 12.

Page 224, *Eighteen and a volunteer*: Gregory Orr, "Eighteen and a volunteer with the Movement," in *River Inside the River* (New York: Norton, 2013). See also Gregory Orr, *The Blessing: A Memoir* (San Francisco: Council Oak Books, 2002) and John Keats, "Ode to a Nightingale," in *Annals of the Fine Arts* (July 1819).

Daughters' Daughters

Page 225, *I look upon myself and other songwriters*: Pete Seeger, interview with Paul Zollo, in Paul Zollo, *Songwriters on Songwriting* (Boston: Da Capo, 1988.

Page 226, *Days before she died, Emily Dickinson wrote*: Emily Dickinson, letter to Thomas Wentworth Higginson, 1886. See *The Letters of Emily Dickinson*, ed. Thomas Johnson (Cambridge MA: Harvard, 1986).

Arrested

Page 228, *Any object, intensely regarded*: James Joyce, *Ulysses* (Paris: Shakespeare and Co., 1922), episode 3.

Page 231, *A very interesting sound might occur*: John Cage interview, in Cole Gagne and Tracy Caras, *Soundpieces: Interviews with American Composers* (Metuchen, NJ, and London: Scarecrow Press, 1982).

Page 233, *This is not pain, this is an interesting sensation*: Ina May Gaskin, *Spiritual Midwifery* (Summertown, TN: Book Publishing, 1975).

Page 234, *new new maze*: Jack Nachmanovitch, *Wow, Frantic Kid* (New York Poetry Department, 2014).

Page 236, *Virginia Woolf wrote of Jane Austen and Shakespeare*: Virginia Woolf, *A Room of One's Own* (London: Hogarth Press, 1929).

Page 237, *The reporter exploded*: *Searching for Sugar Man*, directed by Malik Bendjelloul, Sony Pictures Classics, 2012. Also see Sixto Rodriguez, interview with Bob Simon, *60 Minutes*, CBS News, October 7, 2012.

Page 238, *But what e'er I be*: William Shakespeare, *King Richard the Second*, 1595, act 5, scene 5.

Heart Sword

Page 240, *In medieval Japan there was a woman*: The story of Shotaku, the third abbess of Tokeiji temple in Kamakura, appears in many sources. See Trevor Leggett, *Zen & the Ways* (Boulder: Shambhala, 1978), and Zenshin Florence Caplow and Reigetsu Susan Moon, eds., *The Hidden Lamp: Stories from Twenty-Five Centuries of Awakened Women* (Somerville, MA: Wisdom, 2013).

Further Reading

Music

Adolphe, Bruce. *The Mind's Ear*. Ballwin, MO: MMB Music, 1991.

Agrell, Jeffrey. *Improv Games for One*. Chicago: GIA, 2009.

———. *Improvisation Games for Classical Musicians*. Chicago: GIA, 2007.

Bailey, Derek. *Improvisation: Its Nature and Practice in Music*. Boston: Da Capo, 1993.

Berliner, Paul. *Thinking in Jazz: The Infinite Art of Improvisation*. University of Chicago Press, 1994.

Bernstein, Leonard. *The Unanswered Question: Six Talks at Harvard*. Cambridge, MA: Harvard University Press, 1971.

Bjørkvold, Jon-Roar. *The Muse Within: Creativity and Communication, Song and Play from Childhood through Maturity*. New York: HarperCollins, 1992.

Borgo, David. *Sync or Swarm: Improvising Music in a Complex Age*. London and New York: Continuum, 2005.

Cardew, Cornelius. *Scratch Music*. Cambridge, MA: MIT Press, 1972.

Chase, Mildred Portney. *Improvisation: Music from the Inside Out*. Berkeley, CA: Creative Arts, 1988.

Copland, Aaron. *Music and Imagination.* Cambridge, MA: Harvard University Press, 1962.

Cowell, Henry. *New Musical Resources.* Cambridge University Press, 1930.

Fischlin, Dan, and Ajay Heble, eds. *The Other Side of Nowhere: Jazz, Improvisation, and Communities in Dialogue.* Middletown, CT: Wesleyan University Press, 2004.

Gioia, Ted. *The Imperfect Art: Reflections on Jazz and Modern Culture.* Oxford University Press, 1988.

Lee, Colin. *Music at the Edge: The Music Therapy Experiences of a Musician with AIDS.* London and New York: Routledge, 1996.

Levaillant, Denis. *L'improvisation musicale. Essai sur la puissance de jeu.* Paris: Lattès, 1981.

Lewis, George. *A Power Stronger Than Itself: The AACM and American Experimental Music.* University of Chicago Press, 2009.

Mathieu, William Allaudin. *The Musical Life: Reflections of What It Is and How to Love It.* Boulder, CO: Shambhala, 1994.

———. *The Listening Book: Discovering Your Own Music.* Boulder, CO: Shambhala, 1991.

Menuhin, Yehudi. *Violin: Six Lessons with Yehudi Menuhin.* New York: Viking, 1971.

Monson, Ingrid. *Saying Something: Jazz Improvisation and Interaction.* University of Chicago Press, 1996.

Nettl, Bruno, and Melinda Russell. *In the Course of Performance: Studies in the World of Musical Improvisation.* University of Chicago Press, 1998.

Oliveros, Pauline. *Deep Listening: A Composer's Sound Practice.* Bloomington, IN: iUniverse, 2005.

———. *The Roots of the Moment.* New York: Drogue Press, 1998.

———. *Software for People: Collected Writings 1963–80.* Pauline Oliveros Publications, 1984.

Oshinsky, James, and David Darling. *Return to Child: Music for People's Guide to Improvising Music and Authentic Group Leadership.* Goshen, CT: Music for People, 2004.

Partch, Harry. *Genesis of a Music.* Boston: Da Capo, 1979.

Prévost, Edwin. *No Sound Is Innocent: AMM and the Practice of Self-Invention* Essex, UK: Copula, 1995.

Rhiannon. *Vocal River: The Skill and Spirit of Improvisation.* Hakalau, HI: Rhiannon Music, 2013.

Rothenberg, David. *Sudden Music: Improvisation, Sound, Nature.* Athens: University of Georgia Press, 2001.

Small, Christopher. *Musicking: The Meanings of Performing and Listening.* Middletown, CT: Wesleyan University Press, 1998.

———. *Music, Society, Education.* Middletown, CT: Wesleyan University Press, 1980.

Solis, Gabriel, and Bruno Nettl. *Musical Improvisation: Art, Education, and Society.* Champaign: University of Illinois Press, 2009.

Stevens, John. *Search & Reflect.* Teddington, Eng.: Rock School Limited, 1985.

Stravinsky, Igor. *Poetics of Music in the Form of Six Lessons.* Translated by Arthur Knodel. Cambridge, MA: Harvard University Press, 1942.

Sweet, Robert. *Music Universe, Music Mind: Revisiting the Creative Music Studio, Woodstock, New York.* Ann Arbor, MI: Arborville, 1996.

Zollo, Paul. *Songwriters on Songwriting.* Boston: Da Capo, 1988.

Theater, Dance, and Performance

Arkin, Alan. *An Improvised Life: A Memoir.* Boston: Da Capo Press, 2011.

Boal, Augusto. *The Rainbow of Desire: The Boal Method of Theatre and Therapy.* London and New York: Routledge, 1995.

———. *Games for Actors and Nonactors.* London and New York: Routledge, 1992.

Bogart, Anne. *And Then, You Act: Making Art in an Unpredictable World.* London and New York: Routledge, 2007.

Brook, Peter. *The Empty Space: A Book about the Theatre: Deadly, Holy, Rough, Immediate.* London: McGibbon & Kee, 1968.

Halpern, Charna, Del Close, and Kim "Howard" Johnson. *Truth in Comedy: The Manual of Improvisation.* Englewood, CO: Meriwether, 1994.

Johnston, Chris. *The Improvisation Game: Discovering the Secrets of Spontaneous Performance.* London: Nick Hern Books, 2006.

———. *House of Games: Making Theatre from Everyday Life.* London: Nick Hern Books, 2004.

Johnstone, Keith. *Impro for Storytellers.* London and New York: Routledge, 1999.

———. *Impro.* New York: Theatre Arts Books, 1979.

Rosenthal, Rachel. *The DbD Experience: Chance Knows What It's Doing!* London and New York: Routledge, 2010.

Schechner, Richard. *Between Theater and Anthropology.* Philadelphia: University of Pennsylvania, 1985.

Sgorbati, Susan. *Emergent Improvisation: On the Nature of Spontaneous Composition Where Dance Meets Science.* Northampton, MA: Contact Quarterly Chapbooks, 2013.

Spolin, Viola. *Improvisation for the Theater.* Evanston, IL: Northwestern University Press, 1983.

Tufnell, Miranda, and Chris Crickmay. *Body, Space, Image: Notes toward Improvisation and Performance.* Alton, Eng.: Dance Books, 1999.

Wunder, Al. *The Wonder of Improvisation.* Victoria, Aus.: Wunder, 2006.

Zeami, Motokiyo. *Fūshikaden (The Transmission of the Flower through a Mastery of the Forms),* circa 1418. See the translation by William Scott Wilson. Boulder, CO: Shambhala, 2013.

Philosophy Relevant to Improvising and Creating

Bateson, Gregory. *Steps to an Ecology of Mind.* San Francisco: Chandler, 1972. Subsequent editions have been published by Ballantine, Jason Aronson, and the University of Chicago Press.

———. *Mind and Nature: A Necessary Unity.* New York: Dutton, 1979.

Bayles, David. *Art & Fear: Observations on the Perils (and Rewards) of Art-making.* Santa Barbara, CA: Capra, 1993.

Belgrad, Daniel. *The Culture of Spontaneity: Improvisation and the Arts in Postwar America.* University of Chicago Press, 1998.

Berkowitz, Aaron. *The Improvising Mind: Cognition and Creativity in the Musical Moment.* Oxford University Press, 2010.

Cage, John. *Diary: How to Improve the World (You Will Only Make Matters Worse) 1967–1982.* Los Angeles: Siglio, 2015.

———. *Silence: Lectures and Writings.* Cambridge, MA: MIT Press, 1961.

Huizinga, Johan. *Homo Ludens: A Study of the Play-Element in Culture.* Boston: Beacon, 1938.

Hyde, Lewis. *The Gift: Imagination and the Erotic Life of Property.* New York: Vintage, 1979.

Koestler, Arthur. *The Act of Creation.* New York: Macmillan, 1964.

Leggett, Trevor. *Zen and the Ways.* Boulder, CO: Shambhala, 1978.

Loori, John Daido. *The Zen of Creativity.* New York: Ballantine, 2005.

Maturana, Humberto, and Francisco Varela. *The Tree of Knowledge: The Biological Roots of Human Understanding.* Boulder, CO: Shambhala, 1992.

———. *Autopoiesis and Cognition*. Dordrecht, Neth: D. Reidel, 1980. First published in 1973 under the title *De Machinas y Seres Vivos* by Editorial Universitaria in Chile.

May, Rollo. *The Courage to Create*. New York: Norton, 1975.

Padmasambhava. *Self-Liberation through Seeing with Naked Awareness*. Eighth century. Translated by John Reynolds. Barrytown, NY: Station Hill Press, 1988.

Piaget, Jean. *Play, Dreams, and Imitation in Childhood*. London and New York: Routledge, 1951.

Slingerland, Edward. *Trying Not to Try: Ancient China, Modern Science, and the Power of Spontaneity*. New York: Broadway, 2014.

Suzuki, Shunryū. *Zen Mind, Beginner's Mind*. Boulder, CO: Weatherhill, 1970.

Watts, Alan W. *Beat Zen, Square Zen, and Zen*. San Francisco: City Lights, 1959.

Wilhelm, Richard, trans. *Secret of the Golden Flower*. New York: Harcourt, Brace & World, 1932.

Winnicott, D. W. *Playing and Reality*. London: Tavistock, 1971.

Woolf, Virginia. *A Room of One's Own*. London: Hogarth Press, 1929.

Improvisation in Life and Art

Herrigel, Eugen. *Zen in the Art of Archery*. Translated by R. F. C. Hull. New York: Pantheon, 1953.

Nachmanovitch, Stephen. *Free Play: Improvisation in Life and Art*. New York: Penguin, 1990.

Poetic Improvisation

Edwards, Paul, and Kool G Rap. *How to Rap: The Art and Science of the Hip-Hop MC*. Chicago Review Press, 2009.

Fertel, Randy. *A Taste for Chaos: The Art of Literary Improvisation*, New Orleans: Spring Journal Books, 2015.

Finnegan, Ruth. *Oral Poetry: Its Nature, Significance, and Social Context*. Cambridge University Press, 1980.

Foley, John Miles. *How to Read an Oral Poem*. Champaign: University of Illinois Press, 2002.

Lord, Albert B. *The Singer of Tales*. Cambridge, MA: Harvard University Press, 1960.

Lu Chi. *The Art of Writing: Lu Chi's Wen Fu.* Written in 261. Translated by
    Sam Hamill. Portland, OR: Breitenbush Books, 1987.
Ong, Walter. *Orality and Literacy.* London: Methuen, 1982.

Crafts and Visual Art

Crawford, Matthew. *Shop Class as Soulcraft.* New York: Penguin, 2009.
Dalí, Salvador. *50 Secrets of Magic Craftsmanship.* Translated by Haakon M.
    Chevalier. New York: Dover, 1992. First published in 1948.
Kandinsky, Wassily. *Concerning the Spiritual in Art.* Translated by M. T. H.
    Sadler. New York: Dover, 1977. First published as *The Art of Spiritual
    Harmony* in 1914.
Koren, Leonard. *Wabi-Sabi: For Artists, Designers, Poets & Philosophers.*
    Albany, CA: Stone Bridge Press, 1994.
Richards, Mary Caroline. *Centering in Pottery, Poetry, and the Person.* Mid-
    dletown, CT: Wesleyan University Press, 1962.
Tanizaki, Jun'ichirō. *In Praise of Shadows.* Sedgwick, ME: Leete's Island
    Books, 1977.
White, Minor. *Rites & Passages.* Reading, PA: Aperture, 1978.
Yanagi, Soetsu. *The Unknown Craftsman.* Adapted by Bernard Leach.
    Tokyo: Kodansha International, 1972.

Illustrations

Introduction

Page 8, Viola d'amore by Tomas Andreas Hulinsky, Prague, 1781. In the collection of and photographed by the author.

Verbs and Nouns

Page 35, Ganesh statue. In the collection of and photographed by the author.

Stuck or Sticky

Page 43, Bird-headed man, William Blake, *Jerusalem*, 1804, detail from plate 78.

Page 43, Smiling Avalokiteśvara, from the collection of John and Berthe Ford, "Shadakshari Triad and Other Deities," twelfth century, Tibetan, meas. 34 x 29⅛". Appeared in *Desire & Devotion*, 228. Image courtesy of John and Berthe Ford.

Page 54, William James quotation, photograph by the author, with warm thanks to Maria Kluge. From *The Principles of Psychology* (New York: Henry Holt, 1890), chap. 11.

This Moment

Page 73, "Nothing Forever," by John Marron, watercolor and ink, 2002.

Universal Language

Page 83, Workshop in Seattle, 2006. Photograph by the author.

Bedtime Stories

Page 89, Herzegovinian poet sings while playing the *guslé*. Drawing from Народне српске *(Serbian Folk Poems)*, vol. 2 (Leipzig: Vuk Stefanović Karadžić, 1823).

All About Frogs

Page 110, *The Toad*, by Sengai Gibon (1750–1837), Idemitsu Museum of Arts, Tokyo.

Page 115, *Meditating Frog*, by Sengai Gibon, Idemitsu Museum of Arts, Tokyo. The inscription states: "If a man becomes a buddha by practicing zazen . . . a frog though I am I should have been one long ago."

Page 119, J. C. Brown, illustration to Bashō's frog haiku, 1995. In Hiroaki Sato, *One Hundred Frogs* (Boulder, CO: Weatherhill, 2005).

Page 120, Porch Toad, Ivy, Virginia, 2015. Photograph by the author.

Page 121, Frog playing lute, nineteenth century, American.

Page 125, William Blake, detail from *Jerusalem*, 1804, plate 98: "Such is the Cry from all the Earth from the Living Creatures of the Earth."

Twists and Turns

Page 134, Engraving by unknown artist, from Camille Flammarion, *L'atmosphère: météorologie populaire* (The Atmosphere: Popular Meteorology) (Paris: Hachette, 1888), 163.

Listening

Page 146, Jetsun Milarepa, detail from a *thangka* by Lama Karma Chopal, 2004. In the collection of and photographed by the author.

Rubbing

Page 158, Fingers on fourteen-string viola d'amore by Abbondio Marchetti, Milan, 1830. Instrument in the collection of and photographed by the author.

Mushrooms and Tide Pools

Page 170, Mushroom with Milarepa. Photograph by the author.

Wabi-Sabi

Page 174, Shigaraki pottery, front and rear views. In the collection of and photographed by the author.

Page 176, Shoes. Photograph by the author.

Page 187, Kizaemon Ido tea bowl, sixteenth-century Korean, now in the Kohoan-ji temple in the Daitoku-ji complex, Kyoto, Japan.

Page 187, Pluto's moon Charon, as photographed from the New Horizons spacecraft, 2015.

Page 193, Hólavallagarður cemetery, Reykjavík, Iceland. Photograph by the author.

After-Flavor

Page 198, The Dalai Lama cutting the Kalachakra Mandala in Santa Monica, California. Photograph by Don Farber, 1989.

The Way It's Supposed to Be

Page 210, Urizen, in William Blake's *Europe a Prophecy* (London: W. Blake, 1794), plate 1.

Page 210, Urizen, in William Blake's *The Book of Urizen* (London: W. Blake, 1794), plate 4.

Daughters' Daughters

Page 227, Women's March, Washington, DC, January 21, 2017. Photograph by the author.

Arrested

Page 239, Victory over Mara, from Buryatia, Mongolia, nineteenth century, ground mineral pigment on cotton. Rubin Museum of Art. Gift of Shelley and Donald Rubin. C2006.66.305 (HAR 699).

Credits

Grateful acknowledgment is made to the following for permission to use their writings and illustrations. See the notes and the list of illustrations for detailed references to these works:

The John Cage Trust and Laura Kuhn, for permission to reprint John Cage's poetry.

Rubin Museum of Art, New York, for permission to reprint the *thangka* "Victory over Mara."

Idemitsu Museum of Art, Tokyo, for permission to reprint two artworks by Sengai, *The Toad* and *The Frog*.

Don Farber Photography/buddhistphotos.com, for permission to reprint his photo of the Dalai Lama cutting the Kalachakra mandala in Santa Monica, 1989.

Al Wunder, for permission to quote from *The Wonder of Improvisation*.

John Ford, for permission to reprint the *thangka* "Shadakshari Triad and Other Deities."

John Marron, for permission to reprint his calligraphy "Nothing Forever."

National Aeronautics and Space Administration, for permission to reprint the photo of Charon.

White Pine Press, for permission to reprint the quotation from Richard Clark's translation of the *Hsin Hsin Ming*.

Gary Miranda and Tavern Books, for permission to quote from his translation of Rilke's *Duino Elegies*.

Leete's Island Books, for permission to quote from Jun'ichirō Tanizaki's *In Praise of Shadows*.

Paul Zollo, for permission to reprint the quote from his Pete Seeger interview in *Songwriters on Songwriting*.

Lomography Society International, Vienna, for permission to reproduce the laws of lomography.

Joseph C. Brown, for permission to reprint his artwork based on Bashō's frog haiku.

Gary Ross and Warner Brothers Entertainment, for permission to quote from the screenplay of *Pleasantville*.

Gregory Orr, for "Eighteen and a Volunteer," from *River Inside the River: Poems by Gregory Orr*. Copyright © 2013 by Gregory Orr. Used by permission of W. W. Norton & Company, Inc.

Index

About the Author

Stephen Nachmanovitch is an improvisational violinist who performs and teaches internationally at the intersections of multimedia, performing arts, ecology, and philosophy. He is the author of *Free Play: Improvisation in Life and Art* (Penguin, 1990). Born in 1950, he graduated in 1971 from Harvard with a bachelor's degree in psychology and in 1975 from the University of California, where he earned a PhD in the history of consciousness for an exploration of William Blake. His mentor was the anthropologist and philosopher Gregory Bateson. He has taught and lectured widely in the United States and abroad on creativity and the spiritual underpinnings of art. In the 1970s he was a pioneer in free improvisation on violin, viola, and electric violin. He has presented master classes and workshops at many conservatories and universities, and has had numerous appearances on radio, television, and at music and theater festivals. He has collaborated with other artists in media including music, dance, theater, and film, and has developed programs melding art, music, literature, and computer technology. He has published articles in a variety of fields since 1966, and has created computer software including *The World Music Menu* and *Visual Music Tone Painter*. He is currently performing, recording, teaching, and writing. He lives with his family in Charlottesville, Virginia.

More at www.freeplay.com

Photo by Gregory Nachmanovitch